PEARSON CUSTOM

STUDENT SUCCESS & CAREER DEVELOPMENT

University of Baltimore
MGMT 330
Professional Skills: Custom Package, 2ed

ISBN 10: 1-269-05953-X
ISBN 13: 978-1-269-05953-4

Table of Contents

CHAPTER ONE

Attitude, Goal Setting, and Life Management

Jupiterimages / Thinkstock

The future belongs to those who believe in the beauty of their dreams.

Eleanor Roosevelt (1884–1962)

MyStudentSuccessLab Visit www.mystudentsuccesslab.com for added practice, activities, assessment, and videos.

From Chapter 1 of *Professionalism: Skills for Workplace Success*, Third Edition. Lydia E. Anderson, Sandra B. Bolt.

Objectives

- Define *professionalism*
- Define and describe *personality* and *attitude* and their influence in the workplace
- Identify individual personality traits and *values*
- Identify the influences of *self-efficacy*
- Identify and develop a strategy to deal with past negative experiences
- Define *locus of control*
- Identify primary and secondary *learning styles*
- Describe the importance of *goal setting*
- Identify the impact setting goals and objectives have on a life plan
- Set realistic goals
- Define goal-setting techniques
- Create *short-term* and *long-term goals*
- Describe the importance of setting *priorities*

How-Do-You-Rate

	Are you self-centered?	Yes	No
1.	Do you rarely use the word "I" in conversations?	❏	❏
2.	When in line with coworkers, do you let coworkers go ahead of you?	❏	❏
3.	Do you keep personal work accomplishments private?	❏	❏
4.	Do you rarely interrupt conversations?	❏	❏
5.	Do you celebrate special events (e.g., birthdays, holidays) with your coworkers by sending them a card, a note, or small gift?	❏	❏

If you answered "yes" to two or more of these questions, well done. Your actions are more focused on the needs of others and you are most likely not self-centered.

All About You

Congratulations! You are about to embark on a self-discovery to identify how to become and remain productive and successful in the workplace. The first step in this self-discovery is to perform a simple exercise. Look in a mirror and write the first three words that immediately come to mind.

1. _____.

2. _____.

3. _____.

These three words are your mirror words. **Mirror words** describe the foundation of how you view yourself, how you view others, and how you will most likely perform in the workplace.

This text is all about professionalism in the workplace. The goal of both your instructor and the authors is to not only help you secure the job of your dreams, but more importantly to keep that great job and advance your career based upon healthy, quality, and productive work habits that benefit you, your coworkers, and your organization. **Professionalism** is defined as workplace behaviors that result in positive business relationships. This text provides you tools to help you experience a more fulfilling and productive career. The secret to healthy relationships at work is to first understand you. Once you understand your personal needs, motivators, and irritants, it becomes easier to understand and successfully work with others. This is why the first part of this chapter focuses on your personality, your values, and your self-concept.

An individual's personality and attitude dictate how he or she responds to conflict, crisis, and other typical workplace situations. Each of these typical workplace situations involves working with and through people. Understanding your own personality and attitude makes it much easier to understand your reactions to others' personalities and attitudes.

The workplace is comprised of people. **Human relations** are the interactions that occur with and through people. These interactions create relationships. Therefore, you theoretically have relationships with everyone you come into contact with at work. For an organization to be profitable, its employees must be productive. It is difficult to be productive if you cannot work with your colleagues, bosses, vendors, and/or customers. Workplace productivity is a result of positive workplace interactions and relationships.

Personality is a result of influences, and there are many outside influences that affect workplace relationships. These influences may include immediate family, friends, extended family, religious affiliation, and even society as a whole. This means that your experiences and influences outside of work affect your workplace behavior. It also means that experiences and influences at work affect your personal life. Therefore, to understand workplace relationships, you must first understand yourself.

Personality and Values

Behavior is a reflection of personality. **Personality** is a stable set of traits that assist in explaining and predicting an individual's behavior. Personality traits can be positive, such as being caring, considerate, organized, enthusiastic, or reliable. However, personality traits can also be negative, such as being rude, unfocused, lazy, or immature. For example, if your personality typically reflects being organized at work and suddenly you become disorganized, others may believe something is wrong because your disorganized behavior is not in sync with your typical stable set of organized traits. An individual's personality is shaped by many variables, including past experience, family, friends, religion, and societal influences. Perhaps a family member was incredibly organized and passed this trait on to you. Maybe someone in your sphere of influence was incredibly unorganized, which influenced you to be very organized. These experiences (positive or not) shape your values. **Values** are things that are important to you as an individual based upon your personal experiences and influences. These influences include religion, family, and societal issues such as sexual preference, political affiliation, and materialism. Note that you may have good or bad values. You may value achievement, family, money, security, or freedom. For example, one individual may not value money because he or she has been told that "money is the root of all evil." Contrast this with an individual who values money because he or she has been taught that money is a valuable resource used to ensure a safe, secure future. Since values are things that are important to you, they will directly affect your personality. If you have been taught that money is a valuable resource, you may be very careful in your spending. Your personality trait will be that of a diligent, hardworking person who spends cautiously.

Here is an example of how one's past experience shapes one's values. Cory's parents were both college graduates with successful careers. Cory worked hard to secure a new job. Cory continues to go to college and achieve success at work because the influences from the past impact Cory's values and beliefs in the ability to perform successfully at work. However, many of Cory's friends are

Talk It Out

What cartoon character best reflects you?

not attending college, and many have a hard time securing and/or maintaining employment. For this reason, Cory gets no support from these friends regarding earning a degree and securing employment.

As explained in the example of Cory's values, those values are affecting both career and life choices. These are positive choices for Cory, but negative choices for some of Cory's friends.

Attitude

An **attitude** is a strong belief toward people, things, and situations. For example, you either care or do not care how your classmates feel about you. Your past success and failures affect your attitude. Your attitude is related to your values and personality. Using the previous money example, if you value money, then your attitude will be positive toward work, because you value what you get in return for your work effort—a paycheck. Attitude affects performance. An individual's performance significantly influences a group's performance. A group's performance, in turn, impacts an organization's performance. Think about a barrel of juicy red apples. Place one bad apple in the barrel of good apples, and, over time, the entire barrel will be spoiled. That is why it is so important to evaluate your personal influences. The barrel reflects your personal goals and your workplace behavior. Your attitude affects not only your performance, but also the performance of those with whom you come in contact.

Does this mean you avoid anyone you believe is a bad influence? Not necessarily. You cannot avoid certain individuals, such as relatives and coworkers. However, you should be aware of the impact individuals have on your life. If certain individuals have a negative influence, avoid or limit your exposure to the negative influence (bad apple). If you continue to expose yourself to negative influences, you can lose sight of your goals, which may result in a poor attitude and poor performance.

Self-Efficacy and Its Influences

Let us review your "mirror words" from the beginning of this chapter. What did you see? Are your words positive, or negative? Whatever you are feeling is a result of your **self-concept.** Self-concept is how you view yourself. Thinking you are intelligent or believing you are attractive are examples of self-concept. **Self-image** is your belief of how others view you. If your self-concept is positive and strong, you will reflect confidence and not worry about how others view you and your actions. If you are insecure, you will rely heavily on what others think of you. While it is important to show concern for what others think of you, it is more important to have a positive self-concept. Note that there is a difference between being conceited and self-confident. Behaving in a conceited manner means you have too high an opinion of yourself as compared to others. People are drawn to individuals who are humble, display a good attitude, are confident, and are consistently positive. If you believe in yourself, a positive self-image will follow without effort. It is easy to see the tremendous impact both personality and attitude have in the development of your self-concept and self-image. One final factor that influences self-concept and performance is that of self-efficacy. **Self-efficacy** is your belief in your ability to perform a task. For example, if you are confident in your math abilities, you will most likely score high on a math exam because you believe you are strong in that subject. However, if you are required to take a math placement exam for a job and you are not confident in your math abilities, you will most likely not perform well. The way you feel about yourself and your environment is reflected in how you treat others. This is called **projection.** If you have a positive self-concept, this will be projected in a positive manner toward others.

Envision a hand mirror. The handle of the mirror (the foundation) is your personality. The frame of the mirror is your personal values. The mirror itself is your attitude, which is reflected for you and the world to see. The way you view yourself is your self-concept; the way you believe others see you is your self-image.

Exercise 1   All About You

Describe yourself. Include your personality traits, personal values and attitude toward achieving career success.

_____

_____

_____

Dealing with Negative "Baggage"

Many of us have experienced a person who appears to have a "chip on his or her shoulder" that negatively influences his or her behavior. This is reflected in the individual's personality. More often than not, this "chip" is a reflection of a painful past experience. What many do not realize is that our negative past experiences sometimes turn into personal baggage that creates barriers to career success. Examples of negative past experiences may include traumatic issues such as an unplanned pregnancy or a criminal offense. Other times, the negative experience involved a poor choice or a failure at something that had great meaning. These experiences are the ones that most heavily impact one's personality, values, and self-esteem. In turn, this will affect your attitude at the workplace, which will eventually affect your performance. Consider the following example concerning Cory. In high school, Cory made a poor choice and got in minor trouble with the law. Cory paid the dues, yet is still embarrassed and sometimes still feels unworthy of a successful future. Cory is trying to climb the mountain of success carrying a hundred-pound suitcase. The suitcase is filled with the thoughts of previous poor choices and embarrassment. From others' perspective, Cory does not need to carry this unnecessary baggage. In fact, because of Cory's motivation to complete college, most friends and acquaintances are unaware of Cory's past mistake. Cory's current self-efficacy leads Cory to believe success cannot be attained. Cory needs to learn from and forgive the past mistake and move forward. As self-image improves, Cory's belief in the ability to succeed will increase.

If you are one of these individuals who have had a negative experience that is hindering your ability to succeed, recognize the impact your past has on your future. Although you cannot change yesterday, you can most certainly improve your today and your future. Begin taking these steps toward a more productive future:

1. *Confront your past.* Whatever skeleton is in your past, admit that the event occurred. Do not try to hide or deny that it happened. There is no need to share the episode with everyone, but it may help to confidentially share the experience with one individual (close friend, family member, religious leader, or trained professional) who had no involvement with the negative experience. Self-talk is the first step toward healing. Verbally talk through your feelings, reminding yourself of your positive assets.

2. *Practice forgiveness.* Past negative experiences create hurt. A process in healing is to forgive whoever hurt you. This does not justify what was done as acceptable. The act of forgiveness does, however, reconcile in your heart that you are dealing with the experience and are beginning to heal. Identify who needs forgiveness. Maybe it is a family member, perhaps it is a friend or neighbor, or maybe it is you. Your act of forgiveness may involve a conversation with someone, or it may just involve a conversation with yourself. Practice forgiveness. In doing so, you will begin to feel a huge burden being lifted.

3. *Move forward.* Let go of guilt and/or embarrassment. Once you have begun dealing with your past, move forward. Do not keep dwelling on the past and using it as an excuse or barrier toward achieving your goals. If you are caught in this step, physically write the experience down on a piece of paper and the words "I forgive Joe" (replace the name with the individual who harmed you). Then take the paper and destroy it. This physical act puts you in control and allows you to visualize the negative experience being diminished. As you become more confident in yourself, your negative experience becomes enveloped with the rest of your past and frees you to create a positive future.

This sometimes painful process is necessary if your goal is to become the best individual you can be. It is not something that happens overnight. As mentioned previously, some individuals may need professional assistance to help them through the process. There is no shame in seeking help. In fact, there is great freedom when you have finally let go of the "baggage" and are able to climb to the top of the mountain unencumbered.

Exercise 2   Letting Go

How should Cory deal with the negative baggage?

_____

_____

_____

Locus of Control

The reality is that you will not always be surrounded by positive influences and you cannot control everything that happens in your life. Your attitude is affected by who you believe has control over situations that occur in your life, both personally and professionally. The **locus of control** identifies who you believe controls your future. An individual with an *internal* locus of control believes that he or she controls his or her own future. An individual with an *external* locus of control believes that others control his or her future.

Extremes on either end of the locus of control are not healthy. Realize that individual effort and a belief in the ability to perform well translate to individual success. However, external factors also influence your ability to achieve personal goals. Take responsibility for your actions and try your best. You cannot totally control the environment and future. Power, politics, and other factors discussed later in the text play an important part in the attainment of goals.

Learning Styles

Another element of personality is one's **learning style.** Learning styles define the method of how you best take in information and/or learn new ideas. There are three primary learning styles: visual, auditory, and tactile/kinesthetic.

To determine what your dominant learning style is, perform this simple exercise. Imagine you are lost and need directions. Do you:

a. want to see a map,
b. want someone to tell you the directions, or
c. need to draw or write down the directions yourself?

If you prefer answer *a,* you are a visual learner. You prefer learning by seeing. If you selected *b,* you are an auditory learner. You learn best by hearing. If you selected *c,* you are a tactile/kinesthetic learner, which means you learn best by feeling, touching, or holding. No one learning style is better than the other. However, it is important to recognize your primary and secondary learning styles so that you can get the most out of your world (in and out of the classroom or on the job). As a visual learner, you may digest material best by reading and researching. Auditory learners pay close attention to course lectures and class discussions. Tactile/kinesthetic learners will learn best by performing application exercises and physically writing course notes. Recognize what works best for you and implement that method to maximize your learning experience. Also recognize that not everyone learns the same way you do and not all information is presented in your preferred method. With that recognition, you can become a better classmate, team member, coworker, and boss.

Your Personal Handbook

The main idea of this discussion is that personality and attitude affect performance both personally and professionally. If you can honestly say that you have no concerns regarding personal confidence, attitude, and external influences (friends and family), congratulations. You have just crossed the first big hurdle toward workplace success. If you are like the majority of the population and can identify opportunities for improvement with either internal or external influences, a bigger congratulation is extended to you. Identifying areas for improvement is by far one of the most difficult hurdles to jump but certainly the most rewarding.

This text is designed as a personal handbook that leads you on an exciting journey toward creating both personal and career plans. On this journey you will also develop a respect and understanding of basic personal financial management and the influence finances have on many areas of your life. Self-management skills including time, stress, and organization will be addressed, as well as professional etiquette and dress. Workplace politics, their implications on performance, and how to successfully use these politics in your favor will be discussed, as will your rights as an employee. These newfound workplace skills will improve your ability to lead, motivate, and successfully work with others in a team setting. Finally, you will learn how to handle conflict and work with difficult coworkers.

As we move through key concepts in this text, begin developing a positive attitude and believe in yourself and your abilities. Equally important is that you learn from your past. Little by little, you will make lifestyle changes that will make you a better individual, which will make you an even better employee. It all translates to success at work and success in life.

The Importance of Personal Goal Setting

Everyone has dreams. These dreams may be for a college degree, a better life for loved ones, financial security, or the acquisition of material items such as a new car or home. Goal setting is the first step toward turning a dream into a reality. This important process provides focus and identifies specific steps that need to be accomplished. It is also a common practice used by successful individuals and organizations. A **goal** is a target. Think of a goal as a reward at the top of a ladder. Goals typically come in two forms: short-term goals and long-term goals. To reach a long-term goal, you need to progress up each step of the ladder. Each step contributes to the achievement of a goal and supports your personal values. More difficult goals typically take longer to achieve. Goals provide focus; increase self-concept; and help overcome procrastination, fear, and failure.

Influences of Goals

When you set and focus on goals, career plans become more clear and meaningful. They motivate you to continue working to improve yourself and help you achieve, not just hope for, what you want in life.

Consider Cory's goals. At twenty-two years of age, Cory had only a high-school education. After working as a service clerk since graduating from high school, Cory decided to go to college to become a Certified Public Accountant (CPA). Cory's long-term goal is to finish college in five years. Self-supporting and having to work, Cory set a realistic goal to obtain an associate degree in accounting within three years. After achieving that goal, Cory found a good job, has a good income, and has more self-confidence. Still committed to becoming a CPA, Cory needs to earn a bachelor's degree and has set a goal to do that within two years. This is motivating Cory to perform well.

In Cory's example, as one goal was reached, Cory became more motivated and self-confident enough to set a higher goal. Achieving goals results in continually striving for improvement.

Goals can and should be set in all major areas of your life, including personal, career, financial, educational, and physical. Goals help maintain a positive outlook. They also contribute to creating a more positive perception of you and will result in improved human relations with others.

Talk It Out

Discuss one goal that can be set for this class.

How to Set Goals

As explained earlier, achieving short- and long-term goals is like climbing a ladder. Imagine that there is a major prize (what you value most) at the top of the ladder. The prize can be considered your long-term goal, and each step on the ladder is a progressive short-term goal that helps you reach the major prize.

Set short-term and long-term goals and put them in writing. **Long-term goals** are goals that will take longer than a year to accomplish, with a realistic window of up to ten years.

To set a goal, first identify what you want to accomplish in your life. Write down everything you can think of, including personal, career, and educational dreams. Next, review the list and choose which items you most value. In reviewing your list, ask yourself where you want to be in one year, five years, and ten years. The items you identified are your long-term goals. Keep each goal realistic and something you truly want. Each goal should be challenging enough that you will work toward it but it should also be attainable. There should be a reason to reach each goal. Identify why each goal is important to you. This is a key step toward setting yourself up for success. Identify both opportunities and potential barriers toward reaching these goals. Remember Cory's goal to be a CPA? Cory believes becoming a CPA represents success. It is important to Cory, and it is a realistic goal that can be reached.

Exercise 3   Long-Term Career Goal

Write your long-term career goal.

_____

_____

_____

Short-term goals are goals that can be reached within a year's time. Short-term goals are commonly set to help reach long-term goals. Businesses often refer to short-term goals as **objectives,** because they are short-term, measurable, and have specific time lines. Short-term goals can be achieved in one day, a week, a month, or even several months. As short-term goals are met, long-term goals should be updated.

Just like long-term goals, short-term goals (objectives) must be realistic, achievable, and important to you. They need to be measurable so you know when you have actually reached them.

An additional long-term goal for Cory is to buy a car one year after graduation. Cory has set several short-term goals, one being to save a specific amount of money each month. To do this, Cory needs to work a certain number of hours each week. Cory also needs to be specific about the type of car, whether to buy used or new, and whether he needs to take out a loan. The answers to these questions will determine if the time frame is realistic and how much Cory needs to save every month.

Exercise 4   Short-Term Goals

Using your long-term career goal from Exercise 3, identify at least three short term goals.

_____

_____

_____

A popular and easy goal-setting method is the SMART method. SMART is an acronym for "specific, measurable, achievable, relevant, and time-based." Clearly identify what exactly you want to accomplish and, if possible, make your goal quantifiable. This makes your goal specific. Also, make your goal measurable. Identify how you know when you have achieved your goal. Keep your goal achievable but not too easily attainable nor too far out of reach. A good achievable goal is challenging, yet attainable and realistic. Relevant personal goals have meaning to its owner. The goal should belong to you, and you should have (or have access to) the appropriate resources to accomplish the goal. Finally, **SMART goals** are time-based. Attaching a specific date or time period provides a time frame for achieving the goal. For example, instead of writing, "I will become a manager in the future," write, "I will become a manager with a top accounting firm by the beginning of the year 2018." After you have written a goal, give it the SMART test to increase its probability for success.

Exercise 5   SMART Goals

Rewrite the goals from Exercise 4 into SMART goals.

_____

_____

_____

After you have written your goals in a positive and detailed manner, there are a few additional aspects of goal setting to consider. These include owning and being in control of your goals.

Owning the goal ensures that the goal belongs to you. You should decide your goals, not your parents, spouse, significant other, friends, relatives, or anyone else who may have influence over you. For example, if Cory goes to college because it is a personal dream to be a CPA, that goal will be accomplished. However, if Cory becomes a CPA because it was Cory's parents' idea to be a CPA, this would not be Cory's goal and it would make it harder to accomplish this goal.

Control your goal by securing the right information necessary to accomplish it. Know what resources and constraints are involved, including how you will be able to use resources and/or get around constraints. If your goal is related to a specific career, identify what attaining it will require in regard to finances, education, and other matters. Clarify the time needed to reach these goals by writing them as short-term or long-term goals. Referring back to the concept of locus of control, remember that not every factor is within your control. Therefore, be flexible and maintain realistic control over your goal.

Creating a Life Plan

Identifying goals contribute to the creation of a **life plan.** A life plan is a written document that identifies goals in all areas of your life, including your career and personal life (social, spiritual, financial, and activities).

Consider the following life issues:

- *Education and career:* Degree attainment, advanced degrees, job titles, specific employers.
- *Social and spiritual:* Marriage, family, friends, religion.
- *Financial:* Home ownership, car ownership, investments.
- *Activities:* Travel, hobbies, life experiences.

Create goals for each of these major life areas and note that some of your goals may blend into two or more areas. Some younger students are uncertain of their career goals. Others may feel overwhelmed that they have a life goal but perhaps lack the necessary resources to accomplish a goal. Goals can change over time. Stay focused but flexible. What is important is that you establish goals that reflect your values.

Just as your personal life goals and career goals are important, education is an important key to achieving your life plan. Consider the degrees/certificates required, the time frame, the financial resources, and the support network you will require for educational success.

No one can ever take your knowledge away from you. Make college course choices based upon your desired educational goals. Choose courses that will benefit you, help you explore new concepts, and challenge you. To be successful in your career, it is important to enjoy what you do. Select a career that supports your short-term and long-term goals.

When planning your career consider:

- Why your selected career is important to you.
- What resources are needed to achieve your career goals.
- How you will know you have achieved career success.

People choose careers for different reasons, including earning power, status, intellect, values, and self-satisfaction. If there is a career center available at your college, take time to visit and explore the various resources it offers. There are also several personality and career interest tests you can take that will help you determine your potential career. One popular and useful career assessment is the Golden Personality Type Profiler. The Golden Profiler is a well-respected personality assessment that assists users in identifying behaviors that support specific careers. Additional career assessments are offered at many college career centers and online. These useful assessments help identify interests, abilities, and

Web Quiz

Discover your personality

Take the Golden Personality Type Profiler or search for another online personality test to take.

www.mystudentsuccesslab.com.

personality traits to determine which career will suit you best. Use all resources available and gather information to assist you in making the best career decision. Conduct Internet searches, interview people who are already working in your field of interest, perform an internship, volunteer, or job shadow in a field that interests you. Doing so will help clarify your goals and life plan. An additional discussion on career exploration is presented in a later chapter.

Consider the type of personal relationships you want in the future. Goals should reflect your choice of marriage, family, friends, and religion. Identify where you want to be financially. Many people dream of becoming a millionaire, but you need to be realistic. Think about what kind of house you want to live in and what type of car you want to drive. If a spouse and children are in your future, account for their financial needs, as well. Also identify what outside activities you enjoy, including hobbies and travel. The personal financial plan you create will be a part of achieving these goals. Think about what results and rewards will come from achieving your goals.

Intrinsic rewards include such things as self-satisfaction and pride of accomplishment. These come from within you and are what you value in life. **Extrinsic rewards** include such things as money and praise. These rewards come from external sources. Intrinsic and extrinsic rewards are needed to achieve satisfaction in your future. Both are equally important and should be recognized. They motivate you and help you maintain a positive outlook when working toward goals.

Priorities

Priorities determine what needs to be done and in what order. Properly managing priorities is the key to reaching goals. Not only is it important in your personal life, but it will be necessary at work.

You may need to adjust priorities to reach your goals. Before priorities can be placed in order, determine what they are. Sometimes your first priority is not necessarily what is most important in life; it is just that a particular activity demands the most attention at a specific point in time. For example, if Cory has a young child, that child is one of the most important things in Cory's life. However, if Cory is attending college to become a CPA and needs an evening to study for a big exam, the priority will be to study for the exam. That does not mean the exam is more important than the child. However, passing the exam is a step toward a better future for Cory and the child.

Cory's decision is called a **trade-off.** A trade-off is giving up one thing to do something else. Another example involving Cory is the decision to purchase a car in one year; Cory needs to save a certain amount of money each month. In order to do this, Cory may have to give up going to the coffee shop each morning and instead make coffee at home in order to set aside enough money to meet the savings goal to purchase the car.

Life plans require flexibility. When working toward goals, be flexible. Times change, technology changes, and priorities may change, which influence your goals. Reevaluate goals at least once a year. You may need to update or revise your goals and/or time lines more frequently than once a year because a situation changed. If that is the case, be flexible and update the goals. Do not abandon your goals because the situation changed.

Talk It Out

Share common rewards that are important to you. Identify these rewards as intrinsic or extrinsic.

Talk It Out

Identify priorities and trade-offs for successfully completing this course.

Workplace Dos and Don'ts

Do realize the impact your personality has on overall workplace performance	*Don't* assume that everyone thinks and behaves like you
Do believe that you are a talented, capable human being. Project self-confidence	*Don't* become obsessed with how others view you. Be and do your best
Do let go of past baggage	*Don't* keep telling everyone about a past negative experience
Do set goals in writing	*Don't* set goals that are impossible to reach
Do set long-term and short-term goals	*Don't* give up on goals
Do make your goals attainable	*Don't* wait to create goals
Do have measurable goals	*Don't* create unrealistic goals
Do set priorities. Include trade-offs and flexibility when setting goals	*Don't* give up when working to reach your goals

Concept Review and Application

Summary of Key Concepts

- How you view yourself dictates how you treat others and what type of employee you will be
- Your views of yourself, your environment, and your past experiences comprise your personality, values, attitude, and self-efficacy
- Negative past experiences create unnecessary baggage that either delays or prevents you from reaching your goals. Acknowledge and begin dealing with these negative experiences

- There are three primary learning styles: visual, auditory, and tactile/kinesthetic (sight, sound, and touch). Individuals must recognize how they best learn and also be aware that others may or may not share their same learning style
- Goal setting is important in helping you keep focused. It will increase your self-concept and help you become more successful in all areas of your life
- As goals are reached, motivation and self-confidence will increase
- Goals need to be put into writing. They need to be realistic and measurable. Know who owns the goals and who controls the goals. A time frame is needed to know when you plan on reaching these goals
- Long-term goals are set to be achieved in five to ten years
- Short-term goals are achieved within a year's time and are needed to reach long-term goals
- When creating a life plan, consider all aspects of your life, including personal, career, and education
- Flexibility and properly managing priorities are needed to successfully achieve goals
- As you begin a new job, establish a relationship with a mentor

Key Terms

attitude	extrinsic rewards	goal
human relations	intrinsic rewards	learning style
life plan	locus of control	long-term goals
mirror words	objectives	personality
priorities	professionalism	projection
self-concept	self-efficacy	self-image
short-term goals	SMART goal	trade-off
values		

If You Were the Boss

1. How would you deal with an employee who displays poor self-efficacy?
2. How would recognizing different learning styles help you be a better boss?
3. Why does an employer need to set goals?
4. Why is it important that an employer ensure that employees set personal and career goals?

Web Links

http://www.humanmetrics.com/cgi-win/JTypes1.htm
http://www.colorquiz.com
http://personality-project.org/personality.html
http://www.ncrel.org/sdrs/areas/issues/students/learning/lr2locus.htm
http://www.mindtools.com/pages/article/newHTE_06.htm
http://www.topachievement.com/goalsetting.html
http://www.mygoals.com/helpGoalsettingTips.html
http://www.gems4friends.com/goals/index.html

Activities

Activity 1

Apply the learning styles discussed in this chapter and complete the following statements.

In the classroom, I learn best by

_____

In the classroom, I have difficulty learning when

_____

How will you use this information to perform better?

_____

Activity 2

Write down four words to describe your ideal self-concept.

1. _____

2. _____

3. _____

4. _____

What steps are necessary to make your ideal self-concept a reality?

_____

_____

Activity 3

What outside experiences and/or influences affect your educational behavior?

Outside Experiences and/or Influences.
1.
2.
3.
4.

Activity 4

Share the following information to introduce yourself to your classmates.

1. What is your name?

_____

2. Where were you born?

_____

3. What is your major (if you don't have one, what interests are you pursuing at school)?

_____

4. What is your favorite color?

_____

5. What is your favorite thing about attending school?

_____

6. If you could be any animal, what would it be and why?

_____

7. What else would you like us to know about you?

_____

Activity 5

Create three long-term goals in each section of your life plan. Make them realistic.

Personal	Career	Education
1.	1.	1.
2.	2.	2.
3.	3.	3.

Activity 6

Using the previous activities in this chapter, set long- and short-term goals. The star is your long-term goal. The steps are your short-term goals. Write positively and in detail. Set one personal goal and one career goal. Keep short-term goals specific, measurable, and realistic. Include what (the goal), when (specific time you plan to achieve it), and how to get there (be specific). Hint: Refer back to Cory's goal to obtain a car.

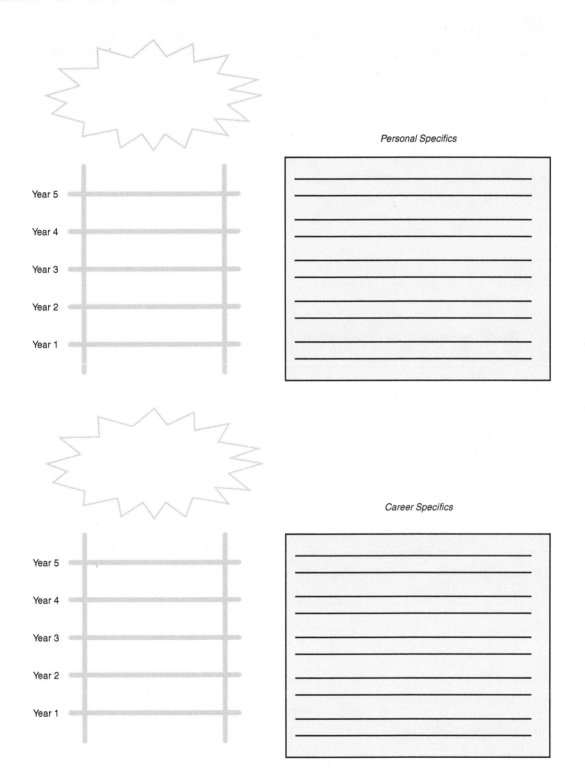

Year 5

Year 4

Year 3

Year 2

Year 1

Personal Specifics

Year 5

Year 4

Year 3

Year 2

Year 1

Career Specifics

1. The _____ identifies who you believe controls your future.

2. _____ is an individual's perception of how he or she views himself or herself, while _____ _____ is one's belief of how others view him or her.

3. When one understands one's own _____ and _____, it is much easier to understand reactions to others' actions.

4. A/An _____ affects group performance, which, in turn, impacts organizational performance.

5. Dealing with negative baggage involves _____ your past, _____, and moving _____ _____.

6. Past influences shape our _____

7. Goals need to be set so you can become _____.

8. Long-term goals are set to be reached after _____.

9. Short-term goals should usually be reached _____.

10. _____ help you reach long-term goals.

11. When setting a goal, there must be a time frame; it must be _____ _____ and _____.

12. _____ will help you decide what needs to be done and in what order.

13. To give up one thing for another is known as a/an _____.

14. Goals should be challenging but _____.

15. It is important to put goals into _____.

16. When creating a life plan, consider the following three areas:

_____

_____

_____

Career Goal Setting

This writing assignment guides you through the process of creating goals. Remember that these goals must be realistic, attainable, important to you, and measurable. Be as specific as possible in every paragraph.

Identify and write your five-year and one-year career goals here. Identify what kind of job and what title you want, in what city you want to work, whom you want to work for, and why you chose this goal. Use the SMART method.

Five-Year Goal

Paragraph 1:	*In five years, I want to be . . .*

One-Year Goal(s)

Paragraph 2:	*In order to reach my five-year goal, I need to set the following short-term goals:*
	Identify necessary steps to reach your five-year goal. Be specific with activities, resources, and time frames.
Paragraph 3:	*I am currently...*
	What are you currently doing to reach these short-term goals? Be specific with activities, resources, and time frames.
Paragraph 4:	*I will know I have reached these goals when...*
	Goals must be measurable. How will you know when you have reached each short-term goal? Be specific with activities, resources, and time frames.
Paragraph 5:	*I need the following resources to reach my goal:*
	Identify physical, financial, emotional, and social resources and where they will come from.
Paragraph 6:	*My priorities for reaching my goals are:*
	Have priorities set for reaching your goals. Include your trade-offs and the areas where you may need to be flexible.

Rotter, J. B. "Generalized Expectancies for Internal versus External Control of Reinforcement." *Psychological Monographs*, Vol. 80, No. 1 (1966): 1–28.

Taylor, M. "Does Locus of Control Predict Young Adult Conflict Strategies with Superiors? An Examination of Control Orientation and the Organizational Communication Conflict Instrument." *North American Journal of Psychology*, Vol. 12, No. 3 (2010): 445–458.

Anderson, C. R. and Schneider, C. E. "Locus of Control, Leader Behavior and Leader Performance among Management Students." *Academy of Management Journal*, Vol. 21, No. 4 (1978): 690–698, doi:10.2307/255709

Bandura, A. "Self-efficacy". In V. S. Ramachaudran (Ed.), *Encyclopedia of Human Behavior*, Vol. 4 (New York: Academic Press 1994), pp. 71–81.

Bandura, A. "Human Agency in Social Cognitive Theory." *American Psychologist*, Vol. 44, No. 9 (1989): 1175–1184.

"Work-Family Conflicts Affect Employees at All Income Levels," *HR Focus* 87 (April 2010): 9.

Golden, E. Organizational Renewal Associates. 1971. Golden LLC, May 2011, www.goldenllc.com

Isabel Briggs, M. Introduction to Type: A Guide to Understanding Your Results on the Myers-Briggs Type Indicator (Mountain View, CA: CPP, Inc., 1998).

O'Reilly, C. A., III, Chatman, J., and Caldwell, D. F. "People and Organizational Culture: A Profile Comparison Approach to Assessing Person-Organization Fit." *The Academy of Management Journal*, Vol. 34, No. 3 (September 1991): 487–516.

Hoel, H., Glasco, L., Hetland, J., Cooper, C. L., and Einarsen, S. "Leadership Styles as Predictors of Self-reported and Observed Workplace Bullying." *British Journal of Management*, Vol. 21, No. 2 (2010): 453–468.

Newhouse, N. "Implications of Attitude and Behavior Research for Environmental Conservation." *Journal of Environmental Education*, Vol. 22, No. 1 (Fall 1990): 26–32.

Doran, G. T. "There's a S.M.A.R.T. Way to Write Management's Goals and Objectives." *Management Review*, Vol. 70, No. 11 (AMA FORUM, 1981): 35–36.

Platt, G. "SMART Objectives: What They Mean and How to Set Them." *Training Journal* (August 2002): 23.

CHAPTER TWO
Communication

Andresr / Shutterstock.comPearson Education

> You can have brilliant ideas, but if you can't get them across, your ideas won't get you anywhere.
>
> Lee Iacocca (b. 1924)

MyStudentSuccessLab Visit www.mystudentsuccesslab.com for added practice, activities, assessment, and videos.

From Chapter 9 of *Professionalism: Skills for Workplace Success*, Third Edition. Lydia E. Anderson, Sandra B. Bolt.

Objectives

- Define the impact effective *communication* has in the workplace
- Name the key elements of the communication process
- Name the three types of communication media
- Describe the dangers of becoming emotional at work
- Demonstrate proper formatting for *business letters* and *memos*
- Demonstrate basic telecommunication etiquette

How-Do-You-Rate

	Have you mastered workplace communication?	Yes	No
1.	I do not use foul language.	❏	❏
2.	I respect people's personal space.	❏	❏
3.	I do not allow emotions to influence my communication.	❏	❏
4.	I believe I am a good listener.	❏	❏
5.	When appropriate, I send handwritten notes to coworkers.	❏	❏

If you answered "yes" to four or more of these questions, you are well on your way to mastering workplace communication. Communication success begins by presenting your message in a professional manner and focusing on the needs of the receiver.

Communication at Work

Meetings, e-mails, texts, presentations, and informal discussions in the hallway play an important role in business and require proper attention and protocol. Employees who have a basic understanding of how to effectively and appropriately communicate in the workplace are at a significant advantage. Knowing what, when, and how to communicate creates a positive impression on others and helps you achieve your objective. Effective professional and electronic communication is vital to workplace success.

Workplace Communication and Its Channels

Imagine going to work, sitting at your desk, and for one day sending and receiving no communication. If there were no face-to-face contact, no phones, no e-mails, no text messages, no meetings, and no memos to receive or write, business would come to a complete standstill. Even if you are talented at your job, if you cannot communicate with others, you will not succeed, much less keep a job. This chapter discusses the process and importance of effective communication in the workplace and provides information on how to improve workplace communication skills.

At work, you have an obligation to share appropriate, timely, and accurate information with your boss, your coworkers, and your customers. Improving communication skills is an ongoing process. Information is power. In regard to workplace communication, your goal is to be known as an overcommunicator.

While eating lunch with employees from other departments, Cory listened to others complain about how their bosses did such a poor job communicating with them. The employees complained that they never knew what was going on within the company. Cory had no reason to complain, because Cory has a manager who makes every effort to share whatever information he knows within the department. After each managers' meeting, Cory receives an e-mail outlining major topics that were discussed. During Cory's department meeting, Cory's manager reviews the information a second time and asks his employees if there are any additional questions. Cory appreciates the fact that the manager enjoys and values communicating important information with his employees.

In the workplace, there are two primary communication channels: formal and informal. Whether it is formal or informal communication, you have a professional obligation to share timely and relevant information with the appropriate people. **Formal communication** occurs through the formal (official) lines of authority. This includes communication within your immediate department, division, or throughout the company. Formal communication occurs either vertically or horizontally within an organization. Formal vertical communication flows down an organizational structure (via written correspondence, policies/procedures, and directives and announcements from management) or flows up an organizational structure (most commonly through reports, budgets, and requests). Formal horizontal communication occurs among individuals or departments at the same or close organizational levels.

The second type of communication channel is informal. **Informal communication** occurs among individuals without regard to the formal lines of authority. For example, while eating lunch with friends, you may learn of a new policy. A major element of the informal communication network is called the **grapevine.** The grapevine is an informal network where employees discuss workplace issues of importance. Although the grapevine is an informal source of communication, it usually is not 100 percent accurate. While it is important to know about current events at work, do not contribute negative or inaccurate information to the grapevine. Do not make assumptions if the information is incomplete. If you are aware of the facts, clarify the information. If someone shares information that is harmful to the company or is particularly disturbing to you, you have a responsibility to approach your boss and ask him or her to verify the rumor.

When the grapevine is targeting individuals and their personal lives, it is called **gossip.** Gossip is personal information about individuals that is hurtful and inappropriate. Any time you contribute to negative conversation, you lose credibility with others. Spreading gossip reflects immaturity and unprofessional behavior. Should someone begin sharing gossip with you, politely interrupt and clarify the misinformation when necessary. Tell the individual that you do not want to hear gossip and/or transition the conversation to a more positive subject. You have a right to defend your coworkers from slander (individuals bad-mouthing others), just as you would expect coworkers to defend you. After a while, your colleagues will learn that you do not tolerate gossip at work and they will reconsider approaching you with gossip.

Refrain from speaking poorly of your coworkers and boss. As a result of human nature, you may not enjoy working with all of your colleagues and bosses. You do not have to like everyone at work, but everyone needs to be treated with respect. Even if someone speaks poorly of you, do not reciprocate the bad behavior. It only displays immaturity on your part and communicates distrust to your colleagues.

The Communication Process

Communication is the process of a sender transmitting a message to a receiver with the purpose of creating mutual understanding. As simple as this definition is, a lot of barriers hinder the process of creating mutual understanding and successful communication. Communication is important for maintaining good human relations. Without basic communication skills, processes break down and an organization may collapse. This is why you need to know and understand the communication process (see Figure 1).

Communication begins with a **sender** wanting to convey a message. The sender must identify what message needs to be sent and how best to transmit this message. The sender has several options for sending the message. The message can be sent verbally, in written form, or nonverbally. Identifying the message and how it will be sent is called **encoding.**

Once the sender encodes the message, the message is sent to a receiver. **Decoding** is when the receiver interprets the message. The receiver then sends **feedback** on the sender's message based upon the receiver's interpretation of the original message.

Several barriers may cause the communication process to break down. The first barrier to overcome is clearly identifying the message to be sent. Once the message is identified, the sender needs to determine how best to send (encode) the message in a manner that will be properly interpreted (decoded) by the receiver. If the sender is not a strong communicator, his or her verbal, written, or nonverbal communication may be misinterpreted by the receiver because the message was doomed before it was even sent. The receiver contributes to the communication breakdown if he or she incorrectly interprets the message.

Another barrier to effective communication is **noise.** Noise is anything that interrupts or interferes with the communication process. The noise can be audible (you can actually hear it with your ears), or the noise can occur through

Talk It Out

Identify the noise you experience during class.

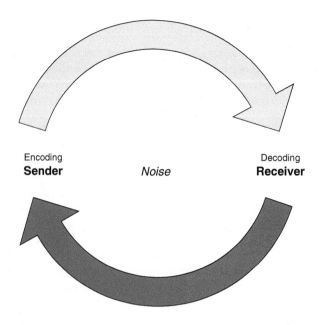

Encoding
Sender

Noise

Decoding
Receiver

Figure 1

Communication Process

other means, such as visual, mental, touch, or smell. Noise may also include emotions such as hurt, anger, joy, sadness, or surprise.

A supervisor in another department really irritates Cory. Cory has never shared this annoyance with anyone. One day, Cory was asked to attend a meeting led by the irritating supervisor. As Cory sat in the meeting, Cory had a hard time focusing on the message. Cory's mind was wandering through mental noise. At the end of the meeting, Cory was embarrassed that there were no notes to share. Dislike for the irritating supervisor affected Cory's ability to listen and be a good receiver. Cory learned a hard lesson that day and made a commitment to be open to every communication, regardless of liking or disliking the sender.

Communication can be complete only if all of the components of the communication process work together to effectively send the message as they are intended to be sent. In order for this to occur, the sender must choose the right medium and overcome noise. The receiver must then be willing to accept the message and provide feedback to acknowledge that the message has been received correctly.

As previously stated, a key element of effective communication is the communication medium (how the message will be sent). Communication media include verbal, nonverbal, and written communication. Let us further explore these three types of communication media.

Web Quiz

Use the web link below, or find another online quiz to identify if you are an effective communicator.

http://ezinearticles.com/?
.Communication-Quiz:—
Are-You-a-Great-Communi-
cator? & id = 32908

Verbal Communication and Listening

Verbal communication is the process of using words to send a message. The words you select are extremely important. If you use only basic words in your communications, you may appear uneducated or inexperienced. In contrast, if you use a highly developed vocabulary, you may appear intimidating or arrogant. If others do not know the definitions of the words you are using, they will most likely not ask for clarification for fear of appearing ignorant. Therefore, your intended message will fail. When selecting words for your message, identify whether these words are appropriate or if the words can be misinterpreted. Use proper English and grammar. Be as clear as possible in your intent and how you verbally convey your message. When people are nervous or excited, they frequently speak at a rapid pace. When you increase the speed of your speech, you increase the probability that your message will be misinterpreted. Your tone of voice also conveys or creates images. It adds to others' perception of you, which either enforces or detracts from your message.

Successful verbal communication involves listening. **Listening** is the act of hearing attentively. Learn to stop and listen. Too frequently, a person will have so much to say that he or she does not stop to provide the receiver time to respond. The receiver's response is the only way a sender can verify that a message has been properly received. Listening occurs not only with our ears, but also through our nonverbal responses. The three primary levels of listening are active listing, passive listening, and not listening at all. **Active listening** is when the receiver provides full attention to the sender without distraction. When the listener focuses his or her attention on the sender, an active listener will provide frequent positive feedback to the sender through nonverbal gestures such as nodding, eye contact, or other favorable body language. Favorable verbal feedback may also include rephrasing the message to ensure or clarify understanding. With **passive listening,** the receiver is selectively hearing parts of the message and is more focused on responding to what is being said instead of truly listening to the entire message being sent. Passive listening is sometimes called conversational listening. In today's society, we have so many inputs trying to attract our attention. As a result, we often get anxious to share our point of view in a conversation and fail to allow others in the conversation to complete their sentences by interrupting the sender. Interrupting is rude and disrespectful. Show others respect by not interrupting conversations. If you accidentally interrupt someone, immediately apologize and ask him or her to continue his or her statement. When a receiver fails to make any effort to hear or understand the sender's message, he or she is in the **nonlistening** mode and is allowing emotions, noise, or preconceptions to impede communication. Sometimes it is obvious the listener is not listening, because he or she either responds inappropriately or does not respond at all. While the ideal is to consistently be an active listener, we know this is not always possible. However, every effort should be made to strive toward active listening.

Silence is also an effective tool used in communication. Silence often makes individuals uncomfortable because our society is used to filling up silence with (sometimes useless) noise. Active listeners need time to digest what is being said and time to formulate a thoughtful response. Active listeners should wait at least three to five seconds before responding. At first, this may feel awkward, but you will quickly discover that you are becoming a better communicator because you are taking time to respond appropriately.

Nonverbal Communication

Nonverbal communication is what you communicate through body language. Even without uttering a word, you can still send a very strong message. Body language includes eye contact, facial expressions, tone of voice, and the positioning of your body. Nonverbal communication also includes the use of silence and space.

An obvious form of body language is eye contact. When you look someone in the eye, you are generally communicating honesty and sincerity. At other times, looking someone in the eye and coupling that look with a harsh tone of voice and an unfriendly facial expression may imply intimidation. In the United States, those who fail to look someone in the eye risk conveying to their receiver that they are not confident or, worse, are being dishonest. Make eye contact with your audience (individual or group), but do not stare. Staring is considered rude and intimidating. Actively work at making appropriate eye contact with your receiver. If your direct eye contact is making the receiver uncomfortable, he or she will look away. Be aware of his or her response and adapt your behavior appropriately.

Eye contact is part of the larger communication package of a facial expression. A receiver will find it difficult to interpret your eye contact as sincere and friendly when your message is accompanied by a frown. A smile has immense power and value. On the other hand, make sure you don't smile when listening

Talk It Out

In what situations is it easy to be in "nonlistening" mode? What can an individual do to improve his or her listening skills in such a situation?

to someone who is angry or upset. He or she may misinterpret your smile as condescending or as laughing at their distress. As explained previously, when actively listening, a nod implies that you are listening or agreeing with a sender's message. Even the positioning of your head can convey disagreement, confusion, or attentiveness.

Another element of nonverbal communication is the use and positioning of your body. Having your arms crossed in front of your body may be interpreted in several ways. You could be physically cold, angry, or uninterested. When you are not physically cold, having your arms crossed implies that you are creating a barrier between yourself and the other person. To eliminate any miscommunication, it is best to have your arms at your sides. Do not hide your hands in your pockets. In speaking with others, be aware of the positioning of your arms and those of your audience. Also, be aware of the positioning of your entire body. Turn your body toward those to whom you are speaking. It is considered rude to turn your back to or ignore someone when he or she is speaking. In this case, you are using your entire body to create a barrier. Avoid this type of rude behavior. This only communicates immaturity on your part.

Exercise 1   Body Language

With a partner, take turns communicating the following emotions through body language.

Emotion	Signal
1. Concern	
2. Distrust	
3. Eagerness	
4. Boredom	
5. Self-importance	

The use of your hands is extremely important in effective communication. Through varied positioning, you can use your hands to nonverbally ask someone to stop a behavior, be quiet, or reprimand him or her. Be aware of the positioning of your hands and fingers. In the United States, it is considered rude to point at someone with one finger. Many finger and hand gestures commonly used in the United States are quite offensive in other countries. If you have nervous gestures such as popping your knuckles, biting your nails, or continually tapping your fingers, take steps to eliminate these habits.

Apart from a professional handshake, touching another person at work is not acceptable. People in our society frequently place a hand on another's shoulder as a show of support. However, others could interpret that hand on the shoulder as a threat or sexual advance. Therefore, keep your hands to yourself.

Proxemics is the study of distance (space) between individuals and is also an important factor in body language. An individual's personal space is about one and one-half feet around him or her. The appropriate social space is four feet from an individual. Standing too close may be interpreted as intimidation or may imply intimacy. Neither is appropriate for the workplace. However, distancing yourself too far from someone may imply your unwillingness to communicate. Be aware of the space you allow between you and your receiver.

Another element that affects nonverbal communication is emotion. Make every attempt to not become emotional at work. However, reality may cause you to express emotions that oftentimes cannot be controlled. Try to control your emotions in public. If you feel you are beginning to cry or have an outburst of anger, excuse yourself. Find a private area and deal with your emotion. If you are crying or distraught, splash water on your face and regain control of your emotions. If you are getting angry, assess why you are angry, control your anger, and then create a strategy to regain control of how best to handle the situation in a professional manner. Any overt display of anger in the workplace is inappropriate, can damage workplace relationships, and could potentially jeopardize your job. When you become emotional at work, you lose your ability to logically deal with situations and risk losing your credibility and the trust of others. Practice effective stress management and think before you respond. Finally, recall our earlier discussion on the appropriate use of silence. Silence is perhaps one of the most important communication tools you have. Silence communicates to your audience that you are listening and are allowing the other party consideration. Not immediately responding to a message provides the sender time to clarify or rephrase a message.

There are many variables involved in effective nonverbal communication. Interpret body language within its entire context. For example, if you are communicating with a colleague with whom you have a positive working relationship and your coworker crosses his or her arms, your coworker is most likely cold. Consider the entire package: environment, relationship, and situation.

Written Communication

Writing is an important element of effective workplace communication. **Written communication** is a form of business communication that is printed, handwritten, or sent electronically. Because the receiver of your message will not have verbal and nonverbal assistance in interpreting your written message, take great care to ensure that the correct message is being communicated. You are normally not present when a written message is received; therefore, the receiver will be drawing additional conclusions about you based upon the grammar, vocabulary, and presentation used in your written communication.

As you advance in responsibility within an organization, you will be required to conduct an increasing amount of written communication, including formal business letters, memos, and e-mail messages. You may also have the opportunity to communicate through instant messaging, texting, blogs, or wikis, discussed more in chapter 10. Written business correspondence represents not only your professionalism and intelligence, but also your organizational abilities. Consistently present written correspondence in a professional manner. Make all written communication error-free by proofreading the message prior to sending. Choose words that clearly and concisely communicate your message. The three most common forms of written communication in the workplace are letters, memos, and electronic messages. Written communication in a professional workplace should be keyboarded and not handwritten. An exception to this rule is when you are sending a handwritten note conveying a personal message.

Plan your message for successful written communication. Identify what you want to communicate, to whom you need to communicate, and what desired action you want the reader to take after reading your message. After you have determined what you want to communicate, write a draft message that is free of negative emotion. Written communication should begin with a professional greeting and end with a complimentary closing. If the purpose of your correspondence is to address a negative situation (e.g., complaint), begin with a positive note and then factually address the situation, but do not negatively attack an individual. With all written forms of communication, do not send or write any message conveying anger. A good rule of thumb is to always put good news in writing and be cautious when sending negative information in writing. Put negative information in writing only when necessary.

After you have drafted your message and eliminated negative emotions, review your correspondence and delete unnecessary words. Keep written correspondence short and simple. Do not be wordy, and minimize personalization words (*I, my*) as much as possible. Well-written correspondence not only communicates a core message, but also clearly communicates how the sender wants the reader to respond to the communication. Include contact information and a deadline in your written communication if relevant.

Keep the correspondence simple. Identify and use words that project a more professional image. Know the definitions of the words you are using, and use these words appropriately. A thesaurus is an excellent tool to expand one's vocabulary. When utilizing a thesaurus, do not overdo it, and use words in the correct context.

After you have finished writing your message, identify who should receive the message. Share your correspondence only with individuals who need to know the information. However, make sure you have shared the information with individuals whom the correspondence affects. The remainder of this chapter focuses on common written business correspondence, including a business letter, a memo, and a handwritten note.

The Business Letter

A **business letter** is a formal, written form of communication used when your message is being sent to an individual outside of your organization. External audiences may include customers, vendors, suppliers, or members of the community. While it is still common for formal business letters to be sent through traditional mail, with reliance on electronic communication, many businesses now send formal business letters as e-mail attachments. Letters are to be written in proper business format. Clearly communicate your message and expected follow-up activity to the receiver in a professional and concise manner. Letters sent should be error-free. Proofread, sign, and date the letter before mailing.

Business letters are written on company letterhead. Company **letterhead** is paper that has the company logo and contact information imprinted on quality paper. Companies will have a template of its letterhead for letters sent electronically. Figure 2 shows the correct business letter format. Figure 3 provides an example of a business letter. Please note that a business letter can have various styles, and an employee should follow the company-preferred style.

If a business letter is not being sent electronically, most companies have matching mailing envelopes that accompany the letterhead. Address the envelope with the same information that is in the inside address. The letter should be folded properly. Fold the letter in thirds, starting at the bottom and folding up one-third of the way. Then fold the top over the bottom and place it in the envelope with the opening on top. Number 10 envelopes are normally used for business letters.

(Do not type QS and DS, these are shown for correct spacing.)	
Since most business letters will be on letterhead (preprinted business address), you need about a two-inch top margin before entering the current *date*.	August 1, 2015
	QS (4 enters or returns)
The *inside address* should include the title, first and, last name of receiver.	Ms. Suzie Student Word Processing Fun 42 Learn Avenue Fresno, CA 93225
	DS (2 enters or returns)
The *salutation* should have title and last name only.	Dear Ms. Student:
	DS
	The first paragraph of a letter should state the reason for the letter. If you had any previous contact with the receiver, mention it in this paragraph.
	DS
For the *body,* all lines begin at the left margin. Use a colon after the salutation and a comma after the complementary closing.	The second (and possibly a third) paragraph should contain details. All information needing to be communicated should be included here.
	DS
	The last paragraph is used to close the letter. Add information that is needed to clarify anything you said in the letter. Also, add any follow-up or contact information.
	DS
Keep the *closing* simple.	Sincerely,
	QS
	Sarah S. Quirrel
The writer's first and last name should be four enters or returns after the closing to give the *writer* room to sign (remember to have the writer sign).	Sarah S. Quirrel Instructor
	DS
Typist's initials *Enclosure* is used only if you add something in the envelope with the letter.	bt Enclosure

Figure 2

Letter Format

30

August 1, 2015

Ms. Suzie Student
Word Processing Fun
42 Learn Avenue
Fresno, CA 93225

Dear Ms. Student:

It was a pleasure speaking with you over the telephone earlier today. I am delighted that you have agreed to serve as a guest speaker in my Communications class. The purpose of this letter is to confirm the details of the upcoming speaking engagement.

As I mentioned in our conversation, the date for your scheduled lecture is Wednesday, October 14, 2015. The class meets from 6:00 p.m.–8:30 p.m. You may take as much time as you need, but if possible please allow a student question and answer period. There are approximately sixty students, and the classroom contains state-of-the-art technology. If you have specific technology requests, do not hesitate to contact me. Enclosed is a parking permit and map of the campus directing you to the appropriate classroom.

Once again, thank you for continued support of our students. I and my students are looking forward to you sharing your communications insight and expertise with us on October 14. If you have any additional information, please do not hesitate to contact me via e-mail at S.Quirrel@teaching.com or call me at 123-456-7890.

Sincerely,

Sarah S. Quirrel

Sarah S. Quirrel
Instructor

bt
Enclosure

Figure 3

Letter Example

The Business Memo

Business memos (sometimes called interoffice memorandums) are used internally—that is, when the written communication is being sent to a receiver within an organization. While e-mail is the most common form of internal communication, a traditional business memorandum is still used for internal formal documentation and announcements. A memo includes the receiver's name, sender's name, date, and subject. As with a business letter, include all facts needed to properly communicate the message, but be brief and to the point. Ideally, memos should be no longer than one page. Most word processing software has templates for creating memos. Figures 4 and 5 illustrate one way to format and write a business memo if you are not using a template. As with business letters, many companies have a preferred memo style. Check with your employer to ensure you are utilizing the proper format.

(Do not type DS, these are shown for correct spacing.)	
Start the memo two inches from the top of the page.	**MEMO TO:** Loretta Howerton, Office Manager
	DS
	FROM: Lawrence Schmidt, OA/CIS Trainer
Double-space after each *heading*. Bold and capitalize only headings, not the information.	*DS*
	DATE: January 6, 2015
	DS
Use initial caps in the *subject line*.	**SUBJECT:** Memo Format for Internal Correspondence
	DS
Body—single-space, no tabs, left align. Double-space between paragraphs.	A memorandum is an internal communication that is sent within the organization. It is often the means by which managers correspond with employees, and vice versa. Memos provide written records of announcements, requests for action, and policies and procedures.Use first and last names and include the job title.
	DS
	Templates, or preformatted forms, often are used for creating memos. Templates provide a uniform look for company correspondence and save the employee the time of having to design a memo. Word processing software has memo templates that can be customized. Customize the template so it has the company name and your department name at the top. Make sure you change the date format (month, day, year). It should be as it is seen at the beginning of this memo.
	DS
Reference initials (typist's initials) *Attachment notation*, only if needed (if you attach something)	bt Attachment

Figure 4

Memo Format

MEMO TO: Loretta Howerton, Office Manager

FROM: Lawrence Schmidt, OA/CIS Trainer

DATE: January 6, 2015

SUBJECT: Accounting Department Computer Training

This memo is to confirm that the computer training for the accounting department will occur on February 1, 2015 in the large conference room. Although the training is scheduled from 9:00 a.m.–11:30 a.m., I have reserved the room for the entire morning, beginning at 7:00 a.m.

As we discussed last week, this may be a good opportunity to offer breakfast to the department prior to the training. If this is something you would like to pursue, please let me know by next Tuesday, and I will make the proper arrangements. Thank you again for the opportunity to provide computer training to your team.

bt

Figure 5

Memo Example

Handwritten Notes

A handwritten note is a personal form of communication. In a professional workplace, it is appropriate to send a handwritten note to acknowledge special events in careers or personal lives (e.g., promotion, birthday, or birth of a child). It is also acceptable to send a handwritten note to encourage a colleague or offer condolences for the loss of a loved one. A common purpose for a handwritten note is when you are writing a note of thanks. Handwritten notes are written in pen, on a note card. However, it is also acceptable to acknowledge an occasion with an appropriate greeting card. In some situations it is acceptable to send an electronic thank-you or personal message. Handwritten notes do not need to be lengthy; generally, just a few sentences are sufficient. Acknowledge or encourage coworkers, bosses, and others with whom you work by sending handwritten notes when appropriate.

A thank-you note is a powerful tool for building relationships. When you express thanks, individuals are more likely to continue performing kind acts for you. Send a thank-you note when someone does something for you that takes more than five minutes or when someone gives you a gift. Deliver the note as soon as possible. Figure 6 shows the correct format and key elements of a handwritten note.

> **Talk It Out**
>
> When is it appropriate to send a handwritten message? And to whom?

Include the date.	*June 3, 2015*
Start your note with a salutation and the receiver's name.	*Dear Ms. McCombs,*
Be brief but specific about why you are thanking the person. Include how you benefited from the person's kindness. Do not begin every sentence with *I*.	*Thank-you for loaning me your book on business etiquette. I especially liked the chapter on social events and dining. Your constant encouragement and mentoring mean so much to me.*
	Sincerely,
Use a complementary closing, and do not forget to sign your name.	*Mason Yang*

Figure 6

Thank-You Note

Documentation

One final element of effective communication is documentation. **Documentation** is a formal record of events or activities. Some industries require documentation to track a project's progress or an employee's time for client billing. Documentation may be necessary for an employee evaluation, for advancement, in an instance in which a policy is not enforced, or when an abnormal event has occurred that has the potential to evolve into conflict at a later date. These events may support performance issues, business relationships, and business operations. However, it is not necessary to record every event that occurs at work. Employees should identify a method of recording relevant business situations, such as a workplace injury, an angry customer, or an employee conflict, if needed for future reference to protect themselves and/or the employer. Although there are numerous methods of documenting and retaining important information and events, the basic elements to be recorded remain the same.

Depending on the purpose of your documentation, effective documentation records the *who, what, when, where,* and *why* of a situation. Effective documentation essentials include the date, time, and location of the event. Note the event itself (e.g., who said what or did what). Also note who was present when the event occurred and how witnesses to the event behaved or responded. Documentation can be kept electronically, in a journal, or through minimal notations on a calendar. If the documentation is for billing or client purposes, your employer will provide the documentation format. Whatever system you choose, keep your documentation in a secure, private location. Also, keep copies of supporting memos, letters, or other communications, in a secure location. If you are ever called upon to defend your actions, you will have the ability to easily gather pertinent information.

Presentations

Both formal and informal presentations are a normal workplace event, and sometime in your career you will most likely be asked to give a presentation. As with meeting etiquette, be prepared and professional. Presentations are very rich in media, in that they include written, verbal, visual, and nonverbal communication. A successful presentation begins with a goal. Identify the purpose of your presentation, and ensure that every word, visual aid, activity, and/or handout will support the overall goal of the presentation. After the purpose of the presentation has been identified, an outline of key points should be identified to reinforce the message you want individuals to respond to or remember.

Formal presentations include three elements: the verbal content, the visual content, and support content. Verbal content includes the detailed information you wish to share with the audience. When presenting, do not read directly from the visual content. Summarize and add information pertaining to the content. Speak clearly and at a normal pace using professional and appropriate language. Face your audience. If you are using a screen, keep your back toward the screen. Beware of both verbal and nonverbal physical gestures. Nothing will distract an audience quicker than an overuse of "um," "like," and "you know." Hands in pockets, crossed arms, or tapping feet are examples of distracting physical gestures. Dress professionally, and do not wear anything that may distract from your message. Visual content includes anything the audience will view or any activity the audience will perform during your presentation. Oftentimes, this involves some type of technology, including presentation software, videos, or music. When using presentation software, do not overdo the use of graphics, color, or animations. Test all equipment and software prior to the actual presentation to ensure the equipment is working and the software is a compatible version. Preparation and practice ensure that your visual content and/or activities are the appropriate length. If you are including your audience in an activity (e.g., game), make directions simple and the activity brief. Keep your audience focused, and do not allow the activity to serve as a distraction from your message.

Support content normally comes in the form of a handout. This is a good way to reinforce your verbal and visual message in writing. A popular format for a handout allows the audience to fill in the blanks as you present your message. Without creating distractions, add professional and visual appeal to your handout. As you create your handout, follow the same order as the presentation outline. Check your visual presentation and support materials for spelling and grammatical errors. When you are certain your support content is error-free and professional, make enough copies for each member of your audience.

Formal presentations are an excellent way to increase workplace credibility and individual confidence. With regard to workplace presentations, remember that success is in the planning and practice makes perfect.

Slang and Foul Language

Different generations, cultures, and technology use some form of slang. **Slang** is an informal language used among a particular group. Although slang is not always inappropriate. Slang can be easily misinterpreted by others. Slang such as "cool" or "dude" when speaking in the business environment should be avoided. When sending e-mails and text messages to friends, it is common to use slang; however, slang should be avoided in both verbal and written workplace communications, including e-mails and text messages. Become a more effective communicator in the workplace by eliminating the use of slang.

Your words reflect what is going on in your heart and mind. There is no appropriate time to use profane and offensive language at work. Even in times of stress or at social functions, you are representing your company and must do so in a professional manner. Practice self-control. Attempt to eliminate foul or offensive language from your personal and professional vocabulary. Doing so will rid your heart and mind of negativity. If you utilize inappropriate language at work, immediately apologize. Make a mental note of what situation caused you to behave poorly and learn from the experience. Ask yourself how you could have better handled the situation, and mentally rehearse a proper, more acceptable method of verbally handling a challenging situation.

Potentially Offensive Names

Names that could be considered sexist and offensive are inappropriate in a business setting. Using inappropriate names toward coworkers could expose you and your company to a potential sexual harassment lawsuit. These include names such as *honey, sweetie,* and *sexy.* Even if the individual being called these names acts as if he or she is not offended, the person may actually be offended or insulted but afraid to tell you. Eliminate potentially offensive names from your workplace vocabulary. In addition, do not use gender-specific titles when referring to certain jobs. For example:

Instead of	Use
Postman	Postal carrier
Policeman	Police officer
Waitress	Server
Stewardess	Flight attendant
Maid	Housekeeper

Not Always About You

Closing our discussion on communication, we address one word that often dominates written and verbal communication. This word frequently turns listeners off. Unfortunately, too often, the sender is unaware of its overuse. The word is *I*. Be cautious with the use of this word. Self-centered people use it to draw attention, while others who lack self-confidence may subconsciously use the word to protect themselves. They may not know how to turn the conversation to others, so they choose to stay in a safety zone. When you are using verbal communication, think before you speak. If your initial sentence includes *I,* try to rephrase your message. Prior to sending written correspondence, review your message and reduce the number of sentences that begin with the word *I.*

Exercise 2   Checking for *I*

Take five minutes and interview a classmate about college and his or her career choice. While you are getting to know each other, keep track of how many times your new friend says the word *I.*

Workplace Dos and Don'ts

Do carefully think through your message and the appropriate medium	*Don't* be in such a hurry to send your message that an incorrect message is sent
Do demonstrate professionalism in the formatting, word choice, and grammar in your written communication	*Don't* write and send messages when you are angry
Do express kindness to others with both your words and body language	*Don't* utilize foul language at work or at home

Concept Review and Application

Summary of Key Concepts

- Effective communication is necessary for workplace success
- The goal of communication is to create a mutual understanding between the sender and the receiver
- There are appropriate times to utilize both the formal and informal communication channels
- The communication process involves a sender, a receiver, noise, and feedback
- Listening and silence are effective tools for effective communication
- Thoughtfully consider the right words to increase the chance of successful written and verbal communication
- Because the receiver of your message will not have verbal and nonverbal assistance in interpreting your message, take great care with all written messages

Key Terms

active listening	business letter	business memos
communication	decoding	documentation
encoding	feedback	formal communication

gossip	grapevine	informal communication
letterhead	listening	noise
nonlistening	nonverbal communication	passive listening
proxemics	sender	slang
verbal communication	written communication	

If You Were the Boss

1. One of your employees uses bad grammar that is reflecting poorly on your department. How can you correct the situation?
2. Employees keep saying they do not know what is going on at work. What steps would you take to increase workplace communication?

Video Case Study: Language in the Office

Pearson Education

This video addresses language in the office. To view these videos, visit the Student Resources: Professionalism section in www.mystudentsuccesslab. com. Then answer the following questions:

1. In the opening dialog between John and Regina, what specific advice would you give John? Why? What advice would you give Regina? Why?
2. Did Regina appropriately handle her telephone call? Please explain your answer.
3. Is the dialog between John and Brian appropriate? Provide specific examples.
4. Name two examples of how Brian could improve his language when speaking with Gerald.

Web Links

http://owl.english.purdue.edu/handouts/pw/p_memo.html
http://blog.justjobs.com/using-foul-language-in-the-workplace-can-get-you-fired/

Activities

Activity 1

Without infringing on someone's privacy, discreetly observe a stranger's body language for approximately five minutes. Stay far enough away to not hear him or her speak. Name at least two assumptions you can make by simply watching the person's gestures, movements, and expressions.

Gesture, Movement, or Expression	Assumption
1.	
2.	
3.	

Activity 2

Watch a television news show for a half hour. Document at least two facial expressions of an individual being interviewed. Did the individual's facial expressions match his or her statements?

Facial Expression	Match Statements: Yes or No
1.	
2.	

Activity 3

Review the following letter and identify five formatting errors. How should they be corrected?

April

Sandra Wong, Vice President
Human Resource Department
Robinson Enterprises
55123 W. Robinson Lane
Prosperity, CA 99923

Dear Sandra Wong

It was a pleasure speaking with you this afternoon regarding the average salary you pay your receptionists. This data will be useful as our company begins creating a new receptionist position for our California site.

I am most appreciative of your offer to mail me a copy of your most recent salary guide for all production positions. I look forward to receiving that guide in the mail. As a thank-you for your kindness, I am enclosing coupons for our company product.

If there is any information I can provide to assist you, please let me know. Thank-you again for your cooperation.

Sincerely,
Cory Kringle

List Errors	Correct Errors
1.	
2.	
3.	
4.	
5.	

Activity 4

Review the following memo and identify five errors. How should they be corrected?

MEMORANDUM

Re: Budget Meeting

To: Mason Jared

From: Cory Kringle

Date: May 1

Hey Mason. I wanted to remind you that we have a meeting next week to talk about next year's budget. Bring some numbers and we'll work through them. Bye.

-Cory

List Errors	Correct Errors
1.	
2.	
3.	
4.	
5.	

1. The two types of workplace communication include _____ and

   _____ communication.

2. A major form of the informal communication network is called _____.

3. When the _____ is targeting individuals and their personal lives, it is called

   _____.

4. When _____ are displayed at work, it becomes difficult to think and behave in

   a logical manner.

5. Nonverbal communication is what we communicate through our _____.

6. _____ communicates to your audience that you are listening and are allowing

   the other party consideration.

7. Check that all _____ is error-free by proofreading prior to sending.

Suggested Readings

Gallo C. "Why Leadership Means Listening," *Businessweek* (January 31, 2007), http://www.businessweek.com/smallbiz/content/jan2007/sb20070131_192848.htm

Dan, R. J. (2010). In the Company of Others: An Introduction to Communication (New York: Oxford University Press), pp. 157–166.

Susan, Y. "The New Trend in Communication: Silent Listening," *Salesopedia*. Retrieved May 31, 2011, www.salesopedia.com/index.php/component/content/1863?task=view&Itemid=10479

Paul, P. "Proxemics in Clinical and Administrative Settings." *Journal of Healthcare Management*, Vol. 50, No. 3 (May–June 2005): 151–154.

Carter, L. Ideas for adding soft skills education to service learning and capstone courses for computer science students. ACM Technical Symposium on Computer Science Education Proceedings. Dallas, TX. March 9–12, 2011, pp. 517–522.

Electronic Communications

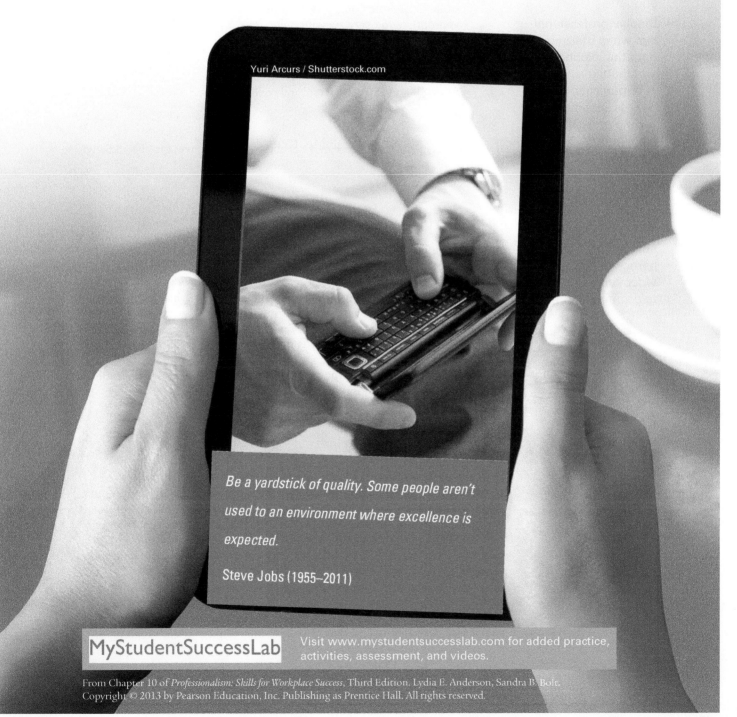

Yuri Arcurs / Shutterstock.com

Be a yardstick of quality. Some people aren't used to an environment where excellence is expected.

Steve Jobs (1955–2011)

MyStudentSuccessLab   Visit www.mystudentsuccesslab.com for added practice, activities, assessment, and videos.

Objectives

- Explain the basics of utilizing modern workplace telecommunication tools
- Demonstrate proper business e-mail etiquette
- Display professionalism when utilizing both the telephone and mobile communication devices (including texting and call behaviors)
- Demonstrate professionalism when utilizing social media tools
- Demonstrate proper behaviors when participating in *video- and teleconferences*

How-Do-You-Rate

	Are you addicted to your smart phone?	Yes	No
1.	Within five minutes of waking, do you check your device for messages?	❑	❑
2.	Do you have to view/check your device at least once every hour?	❑	❑
3.	Do you use/view your device in locations/situations where you know it is not appropriate to use/view your device?	❑	❑
4.	Do you always have your device visible or easily accessible?	❑	❑
5.	Are you unable to go an entire day without access to your smart phone?	❑	❑

If you answered "yes" to two or more of these questions, you may be addicted to your smart phone.

Electronic Communications at Work

We live in a multitasking, fast-paced world that has resulted in technology addiction. The traditional workplace of the past has evolved into a virtual workplace where most people are connected electronically. Today's workplace communicates through venues including e-mail, mobile devices, texting, instant messaging, blogs, wikis, and audio and video conferencing. The more we are connected technologically, the greater the opportunity for disconnected messages. This chapter focuses on electronic communications in the workplace. Due to the frequency and speed of message transmission, those who communicate through today's virtual workplace need to take great care to ensure all electronic communications are sent in a clear and professional manner.

Telecommunication Basics

With the increase of technology in the workplace, the proper use of electronic communication tools, devices, and equipment becomes increasingly important. Common communication tools include various forms of computers, software, e-mail, Internet, and mobile (smart) devices. Employers may provide these tools to employees free of charge. If you utilize company-provided tools (including a computer, company server, or e-mail address), the tools, equipment, and messages are company property. Use these items only for company business. This includes the use of the Internet and electronic messaging. Many organizations have technology-use policies that outline expectations including privacy, liability, and potential misconduct issues. Ensure the messages you send and receive do not violate confidentiality and that they represent the company in a favorable light.

With a wide variety of electronic device options, keep in mind that there are proper times and places for their use. In some work situations, it is perfectly appropriate to utilize a laptop, tablet, or mobile device. In other situations, it is highly inappropriate. Only utilize the communication tool when it is relevant to the discussion or issue you are addressing. The communication tool should not distract from the conversation at hand. When in doubt, ask permission to use the device and explain why you want to use it to assist in the discussion.

Cory was in a company meeting. During the meeting, there was disagreement on whether the company's competitor had specific information on its website. Cory quickly pulled out a smart phone and began pulling up the competitor's website. One of the company executives glared at Cory, assuming Cory was being rude by texting or tending to personal business. Catching the executive's glare, Cory immediately held up the device and said, "I don't want to appear rude. I am quickly checking our competitor's site." Cory quickly retrieved and reported on the site and was able to contribute valuable information to the discussion.

Practice good computer hygiene. If possible, routinely scan your equipment for viruses, cookies, and other malicious coding that can be potentially harmful. Just as you would not show up to work when you are sick, you do not want to be responsible for contaminating others' communication tools when sharing information electronically. Regularly back up documents for preservation should a storage device fail.

Talk It Out

How might Cory have better handled the situation of using a smart phone during a meeting?

The Business E-mail

Electronic mail (e-mail) is the most common form of internal and external electronic communications in the workplace. With e-mail messages, you can directly type a message or attach a business document to your e-mail. E-mail creates more efficient communication within an organization and with individuals outside of the organization.

When sending an e-mail, ensure the subject line clearly describes the purpose of the e-mail message to let the reader know your message is not spam or a virus. Include a descriptive subject in the subject line that makes the receiver want to read the message. Do not leave the subject line blank nor use the words "Hi" or "Hello." It is also inappropriate to use the words "Urgent," "Important," or "Test" in a subject line. Most e-mail software contains a command that tags a message as important or urgent. The common tag is an exclamation point (!). Tag only important messages. A proper business e-mail subject line is formatted the same as a hard-copy memo subject line, which uses initial capitalization of words and no abbreviations.

As with all workplace equipment, business e-mail should be used only for business purposes. When composing or responding to e-mails, emoticons (faces made and embedded in e-mail messages) are inappropriate in business messages. Including emoticons in business messages reduces your professional image. Refrain from forwarding messages that are not work-related. These non-business-related messages clutter up company servers and may contain viruses and cookies. Maintain an organized and updated electronic address book and make every attempt to preserve the confidentiality of your address book.

When you receive a work-related message that requires a reply, respond to the message. Ignoring a message is rude and communicates to the sender that you do not care. You also run the risk of being excluded from future messages.

Writing E-mail Messages

E-mail is a necessary technology in nearly every workplace and can be easily misused. As with formal correspondence written on company letterhead, an e-mail should utilize proper layout, spelling, and grammar. Just like writing a business letter, composing a successful e-mail message involves planning and identifying the purpose of your message. Include what specifically needs to be communicated and what action you want the receiver(s) to take. Your message may be informational, or it may be a topic for discussion, or the message may require a decision.

Identify who should receive your e-mail message and include only individuals who need to know the information you are sharing. When sending an e-mail message, you have the option of sending the message directly to individuals on the "To:" line to the main recipient. You can also copy (cc:) the message to individuals by listing them in the "cc:" line. Any individual to whom the message is directed should be listed in the "To" line. Individuals who are named in the message and are not included in the "To:" line should be listed in the "cc:" line, as well as individuals who may be affected by the message. It is not necessary to include your boss in every e-mail. E-mail software has the option of blind copying (bcc:) your message to others through the use of "bcc:"; when an individual is blind copied on an e-mail, the bcc: recipient can see the main and cc: recipients, but the main and cc: recipients do not see the bcc: recipient. Not all recipients are aware of who is included in the message, and this creates a sense of mistrust. The use of blind copying (bcc:) is discouraged, except in the case of sending an e-mail to a mailing list where you do not want the recipients to see the other names due to privacy issues.

Exercise 1   Create an E-mail

Your boss (Austin@workspace.star) asks you to send a copy of a meeting memo to your coworkers: Charlie@workspace.star, Ben@workspace.star, and Audrey@workspace.star. Fill in the proper entries.

To:	
Cc:	
Bcc:	
Subject:	

After you have planned your message, begin writing a draft message. As you write your draft, clearly communicate your primary message early in the e-mail so as to capture and keep the reader's attention. Include the key points you want to communicate and the specific action you are requesting from the reader(s). Consider the reader's perspective and communicate the message in a positive manner. If your message contains several points, bullet or number each item and/or use subheadings to make it easier for the reader to follow and properly respond to your message. After you have finished composing your message, edit the message. Delete unnecessary words, and review the message for clarity and conciseness. People often judge others' professionalism based upon their writing skills. When you are satisfied, proofread the entire message. Most business e-mail software contains both spelling and grammar check—use them. If your message refers to an attachment, do not forget to include the attachment. Before sending your e-mail, give your message one final review, ensure the proper file is attached (if relevant), and check that you are sending the message to the appropriate parties. Also, review that the subject line concisely summarizes your message. After you have taken these steps, send your e-mail.

When sending e-mail messages practice positive e-mail habits:

- Mark only important time-sensitive messages "Urgent" (!). Marking all outgoing messages as urgent weakens your credibility, as it becomes hard for individuals to identify which of your messages truly are urgent. People may stop reading your messages immediately or altogether.
- Check all outgoing messages for proper spelling and grammar. Nothing lessens credibility faster than receiving a message filled with spelling and grammatical errors, especially since the majority of e-mail software comes with tools to correct them.
- E-mail messages written in all capital letters or with large and colorful letters are interpreted as yelling and are considered rude.
- Business e-mail should not have decorative backgrounds or use emoticons.
- If your e-mail software has the ability to embed a permanent signature, use it. Include your first and last name, title, company, business address, contact phone, and e-mail address.
- Some software has the capability of requesting a "return receipt" whenever a message is read and received. Some individuals consider this an invasion of privacy. Use this function only when necessary.
- If you will be out of the office and unable to access and/or respond to your e-mail message within a reasonable time, utilize an automated response to all e-mail messages informing the senders that you are unavailable. Remember to retract the automated response when you return.

Talk It Out

When is an appropriate time to use the return receipt feature in an e-mail message?

A common practice when utilizing workplace e-mail is that of forwarding business messages. If misused, this practice can cause conflict and/or embarrassment. Forwarding messages saves time and brings parties into the loop on a subject they may have not originally been involved with. When forwarding messages, include only individuals for whom the information is relevant. Prior to forwarding a message, ensure that none of the earlier information in the string of e-mails could embarrass anyone and does not contain information that should not be shared with others. If you are unsure the information has the potential to embarrass someone, do not forward the message. Simply summarize the situation in a new e-mail with (potentially) new recipients and copy (cc:) the original parties if appropriate.

Using business e-mail was a common activity for Cory. Cory was careful to always include an appropriate subject line, ensured that the content was professionally and concisely written, requested an action or follow-up activity, and sent it to the appropriate people. Cory was taken aback one day when a coworker sent Cory a negative e-mail for including inappropriate recipients in an e-mail message. The individual scolding Cory had sent his negative e-mail to everyone in the department, which embarrassed Cory. Cory reviewed the e-mail in question and did not see anything wrong with the message or the recipient list. As Cory reflected on how best to respond, Cory decided that the individual who sent the negative message acted on emotion and embarrassed himself to all of his coworkers in the process of trying to embarrass Cory. Therefore, Cory felt it best to not respond.

Mobile (Portable) Communication Devices

Today's business environment relies on current technologies to improve communication. This is achieved through the use of mobile (portable) communication devices. Common devices include cell phones, smart phones, personal digital assistants (PDAs), portable music/entertainment devices, and wireless computers. While the use of these tools is acceptable in most business situations, employees need to be aware of the proper etiquette regarding the use of these devices. Just as it is impolite to verbally interrupt someone who is talking, it is also impolite to interrupt a conversation or meeting with incoming or outgoing electronic communications. There are two basic guidelines for using electronic communication devices. First, you may use your communication device if you are alone, in a private area, and its use is permitted at your workplace. Second, you may use your device when attending a meeting or business activity and it is necessary for communication. If the use of the device is not relevant to the activity, silence your device and place it screen down on the table, or turn it off and put it away. Do not answer calls. If you are expecting and receive an important call, politely excuse yourself from the room and take the call in private. If you forget to turn off the sound and it rings, apologize and immediately silence the device or turn it off. Although these guidelines are for business purposes, they should pertain to personal use, as well.

In some situations, texting is a valuable communication tool. When you are in the presence of others, a general rule of thumb is to text only if the texting is related to the business at hand. For example, if you are negotiating a deal, you may text your boss to identify terms to present. Prior to texting, inform those present of your activity. Just as with all written communication, when texting for business purposes, the use of proper spelling and grammar is essential. Constant texting and utilizing a mobile device has become a habit for many. If you give in to the temptation to utilize your device as a distraction, you will display unprofessional behavior. Therefore, when in meetings, turn off or silence and put your communication device away unless it is explicitly necessary for the meeting. If not, the mere presence of the device may be tempting and will divert your attention from the business at hand. If you are anticipating an important message, if possible, inform the leader of the meeting and explain the situation and apologize ahead of time for the potential interruption. When the message is received, quietly step out of the meeting to respond to the message. It is rude to use your communication device while dining or attending meetings or performances. It is also not polite to take calls in front of others. Doing so implies that the individuals you are with are not important. When taking a call, apologize for the interruption, excuse yourself, and step away for privacy. Many people utilize text slang, text shorthand, acronyms, and codes in personal e-mails and texts. The use of these styles is not appropriate for business communications. In the workplace, texting should be used only for brief, informal communications, always utilizing proper spelling. Just as with other portable communication devices, it is not appropriate and is considered rude behavior to view and send text messages while with others (including discreetly during meetings).

It is inappropriate to use or display portable music/entertainment devices in the workplace unless the device provides quiet background music appropriate for a professional workplace and it does not disturb others.

Phone Etiquette

The phone is one of the most common workplace communication tools. Phone etiquette, whether land-line or wireless, is something every individual must practice to create and maintain a professional image for his or her company. Because the individual(s) on the other end of the phone cannot see you, it is important to communicate properly through the words you choose, your tone of voice, the pitch of your voice, and your rate of speech.

When answering a call, try to answer on the first or second ring. Start with a salutation such as "Good morning," and identify yourself and the company. Convey a positive, professional attitude when speaking on the phone. Smile when you speak, to create a friendly tone. Speak clearly and slowly, and do not speak too softly or too loudly. If you take a call and need to place the first caller on hold, politely tell the individual on the phone that you are placing him or her on hold. If an individual is placed on hold for more than one minute, get back on the line and ask if you can return the call at a later time.

Taking a call without explanation in the presence of others implies that the individual in your presence is not important. When with others, let the call go into voice mail. If you are expecting an important call and are in the presence of others, inform those you are with that you are expecting an important call and will need to take it when it arrives. When the call is received, politely excuse yourself. If you are in your office, politely ask your office guest to excuse you for one moment while you quickly take the call.

When making a phone call, identify yourself to the receiver. The call should be for a brief interaction unless you make sure the receiver has time to talk. If you expect the discussion to be lengthy, ask the individual on the other end of the line if he or she has time to talk or if there is a more convenient time. When you are having a phone conversation, do not eat or tend to personal matters.

Speaker phones are useful communication tools for specific situations and also require proper etiquette. A speaker phone should be used only when you are on a conference call with other participants in the same room or when you require a hands-free device. Use a speaker phone only when you are in a private room where your call will not be distracting to others in your work area. When you use a speaker phone, ask individuals included in the call for permission to use the speaker phone. Alert those included in the call that others are in the room with you and make introductions. This ensures confidentiality and open communication between all parties. Those using a speaker phone should be aware that any small noise they make may be heard and distracting to those on the other end of the line.

Voice mail messages are a part of business communication. A voice mail impression is equally as important as communicating in person. When leaving a voice mail message, keep the message brief and professional. State your name and the purpose of the call, and leave a return number at the beginning of the message. Speak slowly and clearly and leave a short but concise message. After you have left your message, repeat your name and return number a second time before ending the call. When you receive voice mail messages, it is proper and important to promptly return messages left for you. Routinely check and empty your voice mail box.

On both portable and land-line phones, keep your voice mail greeting professional. Include your name and the company name in the message. Clever voice mail greetings are not professional. Musical introductions or bad jokes do not form favorable impressions when employers or customers are attempting to contact you.

Exercise 2   Create a Professional Voice Mail Greeting

You are the account clerk at Garret and Danielle Accounting Firm. Create a professional voice mail greeting for your work phone.

_____

_____

Web Quiz

Are you addicted to social media? Use the following quiz to identify if you are addicted to social media, or find another online quiz related to social media addiction.

http://www.blueglass.com/widgets/social-media-expert.php

Social Media Tools

Companies commonly use social media tools such as Facebook, video/photo file sharing, blogs, and micro-blogs for marketing purposes. Some companies hire professionals to maintain and manage their image through social media outlets. While it may be tempting to post a video or vent about an irate customer, coworker, or administrator online, such behavior is not only unprofessional, but could be a violation of the company's technology-use policy. The behavior could also pose potential legal issues for both you and your employer. An increasing number of employers consider any employee use of social media that reflects poorly on the employer as a violation of its technology-use policy. Individuals using social media for personal reasons need to separate personal sharing from professional sharing. Many organizations regard the posting of company-related information by employees as divulging confidential or competitive information. Regardless of your company's policy, it is best to refrain from identifying and/or speaking poorly of the company, employees, vendors, and customers in all social media communications.

A growing number of companies are moving away from e-mail as a primary means of communicating brief electronic business messages and are utilizing wikis, blogs, and instant messaging for both internal and external communications. A wiki is a collaborative website where users have the ability to edit and contribute to the site. Blogs, also called web logs, are online journals where readers are often allowed to comment. Instant messaging (IM) is a form of online communication that occurs between two or more parties in real time. Business etiquette regarding the use of these communication methods is similar to that of e-mail. When at work, use these venues only for business purposes. Proper spelling and grammar and clear and concise communications are necessary. As with all forms of written communication, professionalism and tone matter. View your participation in a wiki as a form of teamwork. When making edits to the wiki, be sensitive to how others are receiving your comments and, in turn, accept the suggestions of others. Your goal is to provide an accurate web page that properly communicates your message. Business blogs are used as both marketing and education tools. The purpose of a blog is to create and enhance relationships, so keep blog posts and comments positive and meaningful. The difference between IM and e-mail is that you are able to identify who is online at the same time you are. Utilize IM only for brief business interactions. While it is tempting to IM individuals when you see they are online at their workstations, remember that

IM at work is not intended as a workplace social tool. You do not want to become disruptive or annoying when utilizing IM. Whatever electronic communication venue you utilize, remember that you are representing your company.

While it is perfectly common and acceptable to utilize social media tools for personal reasons, remember to maintain a positive and professional online image. An **electronic image** is the image formed when someone is communicating and/or researching you through electronic means. It is becoming common to refer to your electronic image as an **e-dentity.** Routinely conduct an Internet search of yourself to ensure you have a clean online image. If there are negative photos, videos, blogs, or other information that reflect poorly on you, have them removed. Maintain a professional electronic personality by utilizing a professional voice mail message and e-mail address.

Cory's friend Gigi recently got a new job in sales that required her to train and job-shadow her manager for the first few weeks. Cory knew Gigi was addicted to both texting and her social media site, so Cory was glad that she now had something to keep her mind focused. During a sales call, Gigi was not focused and was using a company laptop to play on her social media site instead of reviewing sales figures. Gigi and her client stepped away from the conference table for a minute, and Gigi's boss tried to quickly retrieve a figure from the computer. Unfortunately, all the boss saw was Gigi's social media site. To make matters worse, the site contained a photo of Gigi in a crazy pose outside of her new company headquarters, which included the company's name in the picture.

Talk It Out

If you were Gigi and you knew your new boss saw the social media site open on your computer, how would you respond?

Exercise 3   Identify a Professional Personal E-mail Address for Yourself

Create a professional personal e-mail address

Video and Teleconferencing

It is common for meetings to take place through video or teleconference venues such as Skype, WebEx, and Google Talk. A **video conference** is an interactive communication using two-way video and audio technology. It allows individuals in another location to see and hear all meeting participants. A **teleconference** is also an interactive communication; however, it connects participants through the telephone without the opportunity of visually seeing all participants. When participating in a video conference, a computer, a web cam, and a reliable Internet connection are needed. An individual participating in a teleconference requires a reliable phone line and a quiet location. When taking part in a video or teleconference, the participant will receive a designated time and specific instructions on how to establish connection. Follow these basic tips for a successful electronic meeting:

- Plan ahead. Research the venue you will be using to address any unforeseen issue. If possible, arrange a pre-meeting trial to ensure all equipment works properly (including your volume and microphone).
- Dress professionally (if you are visible to other participants). As with face-to-face meetings, visual impressions matter.

- Maintain a professional environment. Conduct your meeting in a quiet and appropriate location. When you are visible to other participants, a bedroom, public place, or outside location is not appropriate.
- Speak to the camera (if you are participating in a video conference). Focus on the web cam as if you were speaking directly to the other participants. Without interrupting or distracting others, feel free to ask questions, take notes, and use hand gestures.
- Avoid distracting noises. Turn off music or any other items that create distracting noises. Do not eat or drink during the meeting.

When teleconferencing, state your name each time you speak. For example, prior to contributing, say, "Hi, this is Ted. I would like to provide a status report on the Phoenix project." Because virtual meetings require a special emphasis on listening, be quiet when others are speaking and do not do anything distracting. Take your turn speaking and do not interrupt. As with face-to-face meetings, be prepared and actively contribute.

The number of technology-related workplace tools continues to grow, as do their applications. While our means of communicating at work may change, the need for professional communication remains the same. Be respectful and concise in your communication and represent your organization in a professional manner.

Workplace Dos and Don'ts

Do utilize company technology tools only for company business	*Don't* violate your company's technology-use policy
Do practice good computer hygiene by routinely backing up documents	*Don't* forget to routinely scan your computer for viruses and other malicious software
Do recognize the appropriate time and place for workplace technologies	*Don't* allow technology to distract from business matters
Do demonstrate professionalism in business e-mail and texts	*Don't* become addicted to workplace technologies by sharing inappropriate messages
Do practice good meeting habits in video conferencing and teleconferencing	*Don't* let the fact of not being face-to-face in a video or teleconference interfere with practicing professionalism

Concept Review and Application

Summary of Key Concepts

- Send electronic communications in a clear and professional manner.
- Many organizations have technology-use policies that address privacy, liability, and potential misconduct issues.
- Do not forward messages at work that do not involve work-related issues.
- Just as with written communication, when texting for business purposes, the use of proper spelling and grammar is essential.
- When utilizing social media for personal use, refrain from identifying your company and/or speaking poorly of the company and/or its customers.
- Maintain a clean e-dentity.
- Practice good meeting habits in technology-based meetings.

Key Terms

e-dentity electronic image
teleconference video conference

If You Were the Boss

1. One of your employees has been sending personal texts during meetings. How should you handle this issue?
2. Many employees are taking photos and/or videos at department meetings and company events. Should you be concerned? Why? As the boss, what should you do?

Video Case Study: E-mail Etiquette

This video presents expert advice on how to communicate professionally utilizing e-mail. To view these videos, visit the Student Resources: Professionalism section in www.mystudentsuccesslab.com. Then answer the following questions:

1. What should be included and what should be avoided in the subject line of an e-mail?
2. In what situations is it acceptable to utilize emoticons?
3. What is the appropriate e-mail use for non-work-related matters?

Video Case Study: Meetings

This video addresses meeting behavior and etiquette. To view these videos, visit the Student Resources: Professionalism section in www.mystudentsuccesslab.com. Then answer the following questions:

1. Out of the four employees, which one demonstrated appropriate meeting behavior? Provide specific examples.

Pearson Education

2. How did technology assist the meeting, and how did technology hinder the meeting?
3. What perception of the company may the client have from the conference call? Provide two examples.
4. Name four inappropriate actions of the employees.

Web Links

http://www.forbes.com/2010/07/27/internet-email-workplace-technology-privacy.html

http://www.helium.com/items/436615-what-is-the-impact-of-new-technology-in-the-workplace

http://www.businessweek.com/technology/ceo_guide/

Activities

Activity 1

Name two specific technology devices that are used in your job (current or future). How are they used to improve communication?

Device	What Use?

Activity 2

Check your e-dentity. Conduct an Internet search on yourself. Is there anything you need to change?

_____

_____

Activity 3

What should you say to someone who is inappropriately using his or her mobile device (e.g., during a meeting)?

_____

_____

Activity 4

Research at least two different smart phones and explain which is best for a job that requires smart-phone technology for traveling (calls, e-mails, texting, viewing documents).

_____

_____

_____

1. The more the workplace is connected technologically, the greater opportunities for

   _____.

2. Many organizations have _____ that outline expectations including privacy,

   liability, and potential misconduct issues.

3. Practice _____ to ensure you do not contaminate others' communication tools.

4. When in doubt about the proper use of a technology device, _____.

5. The use of _____ is inappropriate for business messages.

6. Blind copying someone in a business e-mail creates a sense of _____.

7. It is impolite to interrupt a conversation or meeting with _____ electronic

   communications.

Suggested Readings

Ott, A. "How Social Media Has Changed the Workplace," *Fast Company* (November 11, 2010).

Friedl, J. and Tkalac Verčič, A. "Media Preferences of Digital Natives' Internal Communication: A Pilot Study." *Public Relations Review*, Vol. 37, No. 1 (March 2011): 84–86.

Bernstein, C. A., M.D. "Communication: It's Not What It Used to Be Psychiatric News." *American Psychiatric Association*, Vol. 46, No. 6 (March 18, 2011): 3.

Zielinski, D. "New Regulations Make Social Usage Policies More Imperative," *SHRM Online Technology Discipline*, June 8, 2010.

Rafferty, H. R. "Social Media Etiquette: Communicate Behavioral Expectations," *SHRM Online Technology Discipline*, March 24, 2010.

Social Media Acceptable-Use Policy, *HR Magazine* (December 2009).

Study Links Technology to Poor Workplace Manners, *SHRM Online Technology Discipline* (February 2009).

Résumé Package

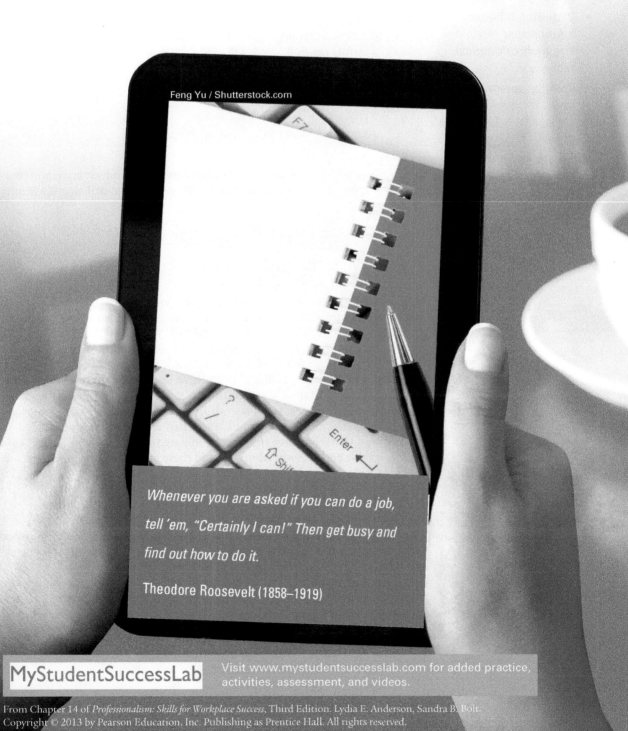

Feng Yu / Shutterstock.com

Whenever you are asked if you can do a job, tell 'em, "Certainly I can!" Then get busy and find out how to do it.

Theodore Roosevelt (1858–1919)

MyStudentSuccessLab Visit www.mystudentsuccesslab.com for added practice, activities, assessment, and videos.

From Chapter 14 of *Professionalism: Skills for Workplace Success*, Third Edition. Lydia E. Anderson, Sandra B. Bolt.

Objectives

- Identify the steps for building a résumé package
- Write a career objective or personal profile
- Distinguish between a *functional résumé* and a *chronological résumé*
- Identify personal *soft skills, job-specific skills,* and *transferable skills*
- Create a winning *résumé*
- Write a *cover letter*

How-Do-You-Rate

	Test your resume expertise	True	False
1.	Paper résumés are not necessary in today's electronic age.	❏	❏
2.	Career objectives are used on all resumes.	❏	❏
3.	Unique skills such as being bilingual or serving in the military can lead to discrimination and should not be listed on a formal résumé.	❏	❏
4.	Using a word-processing résumé template is best when creating a résumé.	❏	❏
5.	If I have a job gap on my résumé it is acceptable to make up a job to fill in the gap.	❏	❏

If you answered "true" to at least two questions, use the information and tools in this chapter to improve your chances of creating and utilizing a winning résumé.

Building Your Résumé Package

Before an employer meets you, they first view your résumé package. A résumé package includes a résumé and a cover letter. Your résumé needs accents package needs to efficiently and effectively sell your skills and communicate how your attributes are unique compared to those of all the other candidates vying for your target job. A **résumé** is a formal written profile that presents a person's knowledge, skills, and abilities to potential employers. Your résumé is an important job search tool that should be continually updated throughout your career. You may not be planning to find a new job or get promoted today, but a time will come when a current résumé is needed. Do not wait until that time to create or update your résumé. As you increase your job skills and accomplishments, add these new skills and experiences to your résumé.

When you begin to create your résumé, you will quickly discover that there are various types of résumés and résumé formats. You may also receive conflicting advice as to how the perfect résumé should look and what it should include. The appropriate type of résumé used depends upon your work experience. A well-written résumé makes it easy for potential employers to quickly and easily identify your skills and work experience.

This chapter will present the tools for creating a professional résumé and cover letter. As you go through the process of constructing your résumé package, make every word, the visual presentation, and the information sell your skills and career accomplishments. There are five steps toward building a winning résumé:

- *Step One:* Career Objective/Personal Profile
- *Step Two:* Gathering Information

- *Step Three:* Proper Layout
- *Step Four:* Skills, Accomplishments, and Experience
- *Step Five:* The Final Résumé

Step One: Career Objective/Personal Profile

The first step in developing a winning résumé is to write a career objective or personal profile. A career objective is a statement that presents your key skills in a brief statement for individuals with little or no work experience. A personal profile is used for individuals with more extensive career experience. Create a career objective or personal profile. Use your career objective or personal profile as the foundation for your résumé. Make your career objective or personal profile specific to the job for which you are applying.

Exercise 1   Your Career Objective or Personal Profile

Write a career objective or personal profile.

_____

_____

_____

_____

Step Two: Gathering Information

The second step in building a résumé is to create a draft document with key headings. This step involves collecting and merging all relevant information into one document. Begin identifying and listing the following information into an electronic document:

1. *Education.* List schools, dates, degrees, certificates, credentials, GPA, licenses, and other relevant education information, including military experience.
2. *Skills.* List all skills you possess.
3. *Employment.* Starting with the most recent job, list the employer, dates of employment (month and year), job title, and responsibilities.
4. *Languages.* List all foreign languages, fluency levels, and if you can read, speak, and/or write the foreign language.
5. *Honors and Awards.* List any honors and awards you have received at school, work, or from the community.
6. *Professional/Community Involvement.* List volunteer work and community service projects. Include any leadership role you took in these activities.

Note that when compiling information to include in your résumé, there is no personal information listed. Personal information including birth date, marital/child status, ethnicity, or religion should not be included on a résumé. It is also inappropriate to list hobbies or include photographs. There are laws that protect employees from discrimination in hiring and advancement in the workplace, and employers should not be aware of personal information unless it is relevant to the job for which you are applying. Older job seekers should not list the date of graduation on a résumé as it could be used for age discrimination.

Exercise 2 Gather Information

Complete the following table:

Education (list most recent first)

School Name	City, State	Dates	Degree, Certificate, Credential, Licenses

Skills

Employment (list most recent first)

Employer	Employment Dates	Job Title	Duties

Exercise 2 Gather Information (continued)

Languages		Fluency (Read, Write, and/or Speak)	

Honors and Awards		Dates	Place

Professional/Community Involvement

Step Three: Proper Layout

The third step in developing a successful résumé is to identify and arrange your information in the proper résumé layout. If you are at the start of your career and/or do not have extensive work experience, create a résumé using the **functional résumé layout.** This layout is used to emphasize relevant skills when you lack related work experience. A functional résumé focuses on skills and education. When writing a functional résumé, list your career objective, relevant skills, and education before any work experience. Include only your high school in the education section if you are using a functional layout and have not yet graduated from college. Most functional résumés are only one page in length. Refer to Figure 1 for the functional résumé layout, and see Figures 2 and 3 for examples of a functional résumé with and without career-related work experience.

Functional Résumé Layout, see Figure 1

Functional Résumé Example with Minimal Career Work Experience, see Figure 2

Functional Résumé Example without Career Work Experience, see Figure 3

Those with extensive career experience should use a **chronological résumé layout.** In the chronological layout, note that the career objective is replaced with a personal profile. General skills emphasized in a personal profile are key skill sets. These skill sets will be used as subheadings in the professional experience section on a chronological résumé. The chronological layout presents related work experience, skills, and significant accomplishments under each respective skill set subheading. When writing a personal profile, include

Talk It Out

Which résumé layout is best for your situation? Why?

Chronological Résumé Layout, see Figure 4

Chronological Résumé Example with Degree, see Figure 5

Chronological Résumé Example with No Degree, see Figure 6

key general skills and key qualities desired by your target employer. Specific skills will be detailed under each respective professional experience subheading. Share major accomplishments and responsibilities from each position. Include important activities you have accomplished in your job. If necessary, add a second page to your résumé. A chronological layout best highlights, communicates, and sells specific job skills and work accomplishments. Refer to Figure 4 for the chronological résumé layout, and see Figures 5 and 6 for examples of chronological résumés.

For both functional and chronological résumé layouts, present employment history and education in reverse time order (most recent job first). When listing work history, bold your job title, not the place of employment. When listing dates of employment, use only month and year. Be consistent in how dates are listed on the résumé.

When you have determined which résumé layout is best for your current situation, electronically arrange the information you have compiled into the correct résumé layout. Avoid résumé templates. Résumé templates can be difficult to update, modify, and personalize.

Step Four: Skills, Accomplishments, and Experience

Once you have electronically arranged your information into the correct layout, it is time to move to the fourth step in developing your résumé. This involves detailing the information listed in your skills, work experience, and professional accomplishments. Work experience includes learned skills, job duties, and accomplishments. Professional accomplishments communicate specific activities you achieved beyond your job duties. Whenever possible, quantify your skills, responsibilities, and professional accomplishments. Do not assume the reader will know what you have done. As you insert professional accomplishments and responsibilities into your electronic file, include both job-specific skills and transferable skills. **Job-specific skills** are those that are directly related to a specific job or industry. If you were to change careers, job-specific skills would probably not be useful. For example, if you are a medical billing clerk who knows how to use a specific software program such as Medical Manager, you will not need to use this skill if you become a preschool teacher.

Transferable skills are skills that are transferred from one job to the next. If you change careers, you will still be able to use (transfer) these skills in any job. For example, if you are a medical billing clerk, you may have learned customer service skills from consistent contact with patients and must practice being positive when dealing with customers. If you become a preschool teacher, the customer service skill of being positive is transferable to the children in your classroom. Employers need employees with job-specific skills and transferable skills, so list both types on your résumé. The term **soft skills** refers to the people skills necessary when working with others in the workplace. Employers want employees that are reliable, team players, good communicators, and able to get along well with others.

When listing work experience on your résumé, include the job title, company name, city, and state where the company is located, and the duties of the position. When listing job duties, be specific with common workplace skills, such as computer skills. The term computer skills can be too general and typically includes many different areas: networking, programming, applications, data processing, and/or repair. An employer needs to know what specific computer skills you possess. For example, inform the employer of your computer skill level (e.g., basic, intermediate, or advanced) with a specific software. When listing your skills, first list the skills relevant to your target job. If you are bilingual include this information in your résumé. Let the employer know what second language you read, write, or only speak that second language.

Résumés do not normally contain complete sentences. They contain statements that sell your skills, qualifications, and work experience. Except for the career objective on a functional résumé, the words "I" and "my" should not appear.

Exercise 3   Detail Your Skills

List as many job-specific and transferable skills as possible. If you do not have any job-specific skills, list the job skills you will have after finishing your schooling.

Job-Specific Skills (Related to Your Career Job)	Transferable Skills (Can Be Used in Any Job)
1.	1.
2.	2.
3.	3.
4.	4.
5.	5.

When applying for a specific position, identify the key knowledge, skills, and abilities the employer desires. General information regarding a specific position will be listed in the job announcement. If possible, secure a copy of the job description. If this is not possible, use the target job information or conduct an occupational quick search on the O*Net database. This database of occupational information was developed for the U.S. Department of Labor and provides key information by job title. Match the key knowledge, skills, and abilities required for your target job with the knowledge, skills, and abilities you possess. Then emphasize this information on your résumé.

Organize your skills and work experience by first listing the key skills required for your target job. When communicating your skills, experience, and accomplishments, write with energy. Use action verbs, also referred to as **power words.** Power words are action verbs that describe your accomplishments in a lively and specific way. For example, instead of stating "started a new accounts receivable system," use "developed a new accounts receivable system that reduced turnaround time by 20 percent." Power words are listed in Table 1 and Table 2.

Exercise 4 Accomplishments

Review your accomplishments and turn them into powerful action statements. Quantify whenever possible.

Choose Your Top Five Accomplishments	Change to Powerful Action Statements
1.	
2.	
3.	
4.	
5.	

Table 1 Skills Power Words

Sample Power Statements for Skills

- Ideal oral and written communications skills

- Understanding of office practices and procedures; ability to operate fax machine, copy machine, and ten-key machine; ability to enter data; ability to effectively interpret policies and procedures; work well under the pressure of deadlines; establish and maintain a positive working relationship with others; ability to communicate

- Accurate typing skills at _____ wpm

- Experienced with Microsoft Office, including Word, Excel, Access, PowerPoint, and Outlook

- Excellent English grammar, spelling, and punctuation skills

- Accurately proofread and edit documents

- Strong attention to detail

- Accurately follow oral and written instructions

- Excellent attendance and punctuality record

- Maintain confidentiality

- Positive attitude, motivated, and organized

Step Five: Complete the Résumé

Prior to finalizing your résumé, ensure that you have added all information identified in steps one through four to your electronic document. As you finalize your résumé, check for information that too frequently is forgotten or not presented appropriately. This is the fifth step in finalizing the information

Table 2	Experience Power Words

Sample Power Statement for Work Experience

- Prepared reports and other materials requiring independent achievement

- Enjoy working in a flexible team situation

- Established and maintained positive and effective working relationships

- Planned, scheduled, and performed a variety of clerical work

- Maintained office equipment and supplies

- Proofread forms and materials for completeness and accuracy according to regulations and procedures

- Processed and prepared materials for pamphlets, bulletins, brochures, announcements, handbooks, forms, and curriculum materials

- Provided training of temporary or new employees

- Maintained department files and records

- Demonstrated ability to receive incoming calls and route them efficiently

- Processed purchase requisitions, ordered and distributed supplies, and maintained inventory control

- Responsibly planned and conducted meetings

on your résumé. The top of your résumé is called the **information heading.** An information heading contains relevant contact information including name, mailing address, city, state, ZIP code, contact phone, and e-mail address. Include your complete and formal name, including a middle initial if you have one. When listing your e-mail address, remove the hyperlink so the print color is consistent. If your current e-mail address is unprofessional, secure an address that is professional. Include only one contact phone number. Whatever number is listed should be active and have a professional voice-mail message. Check the spelling and numbers for accuracy. Spell out the names of streets. If you use abbreviations, check for appropriate format, capitalization, and punctuation.

Immediately after your information heading is the career objective or personal profile created in step one. Review this opening statement to ensure it introduces the reader to who you are and motivates him or her to learn more about your specific knowledge, skills, abilities, and key accomplishments.

In step three, you determined whether a functional or chronological résumé layout was appropriate for your situation. Review the respective layout for proper order and refer to the sample résumés. Confirm that your experience and education are listed chronologically (most recent first). Keep your résumé consistent in its setup, including all periods or no periods at the end of each line, line spacing, alignment of dates, date format, bold/italics, upper- and lowercase words, and underlines. Be consistent with word endings and the use of tense in each section (e.g., -*ing* and -*ed*). Also be consistent with the use of the postal abbreviation for your state (e.g., the state is *CA*, not *Ca.*, not *Ca*, not *C.A*). When your draft résumé is complete, spell-check and proofread the document to ensure it is free of typographical errors and inconsistencies.

As for proper résumé layout and design, underlines, bold, and italic print are acceptable for emphasis but should not be overdone. Do not use bullets throughout your résumé; use bullets only to emphasize key skills. Use easy-to-read fonts and sizes. Times New Roman or Arial are most common. Apart from your name on the information heading of your résumé, do not use more than two different font sizes, preferably 12 to 14 points. Do not use different color fonts, highlights, or graphics on your résumé; use only black ink. It is not appropriate to include personal information such as a photograph of yourself, your birth date, marital status, Social Security number, or hobbies. It is also no longer appropriate to state, "References Available Upon Request" at the close of your résumé. Professional references should be on a separate sheet and provided only when requested. Refer to figure 11 for proper format for a professional reference list.

Tailored Package, See Figure 11

Check to ensure your résumé is presented professionally, is free of errors, and does not contain unnecessary or inappropriate information. Print the résumé in black ink on 8½ × 11–inch, letter-sized paper. Laser print is ideal. Double-sided résumés are not appropriate. If your résumé is more than one page, place your name at the top of each page after page one. Proper résumé paper is cotton-fiber, 24-pound white (not bond or card stock) paper of good quality. Colored paper, especially if dark, is both difficult to read and does not photocopy well. Do not use fancy paper stocks or binders. Do not staple your résumé or other job search documents. Since résumés are frequently photocopied, stapled résumés and other job search documents may be torn in the process.

When you have completed your résumé and believe it is ready for distribution, have several individuals whom you trust review it for clarity, consistency, punctuation, grammar, typographical errors, and other potential mistakes. Remember that complete sentences are not necessary and, with the exception of your career objective, the words "I" or "my" should not be used. Your résumé must create a positive, professional visual image and be easy to read.

Sharing Your Résumé

As you begin to share your completed résumé with both potential employers and members of your professional network, you may have the option of presenting your résumé on résumé paper (traditional hard copy) or electronically (online) as an attachment. Résumés printed on résumé paper are designed to be used for face-to-face job searches. Regardless of which method you choose, the first step is to perfect your traditional (hard-copy) résumé, as this document contains key information you will need to share with all potential employers. When converting a traditional (hard-copy) résumé into an online version, consider content. When forwarding a résumé to an employer or posting your résumé online, such as on a job board, consider key words that reflect your target job. When employers and job boards receive résumés, the résumés are commonly dropped into a database or résumé tracking system that allow recruiters to search for potential applicants based on key words and phrases

Exercise 5   Check for Inconsistencies

Circle the fifteen inconsistency errors on the following résumé.

1100 EAST FAVOR AVENUE • POSTVILLE, PA 16722
PHONE (555) 698-2222 • E-MAIL AERIE@PBCC.COM

AMANDA J. ERIE

OBJECTIVE

Seeking a position as an Administrative Assistant where I can utilize my office skills

SUMMARY OF QUALIFICATIONS

- Computer software skills include Microsoft Word, Excel, Outlook, Access, and PowerPoint
- Knowledge of Multi-line telephone system, filing, data entry, formatting of documents and reports, and operation of office equipment.
- Excellent interpersonal skills and polished office etiquette.
- written and oral communication skills
- Typing skills at 50 WPM
- Bilingual in English/Spanish (speaking)

EDUCATION

Reese Community College, Postville, PA Currently pursuing AA Degree in Office Occupations.

Calvin Institute of Technology, Cambridge, OH Office Technology Certificate Spring 2010

WORK AND VOLUNTEER EXPERIENCE

01/11 – Present   *Rigal Entertainment Group*   Postville, CA
Usher – Responsible for ensuring payment of services. Answer customer inquiries. Collect and count ticket stubs.

11/07 – 02/09   Lablaws   Cambridge, OH
Cashier – Operated cash register, stocking, assisting customers

01/07 – 04/07   Jolene's Diner   Cambridge, OH
Server – Provided customer service by waiting tables, cleaned, and operated cash register

that match the position they are trying to fill. Sometimes, when posting an online résumé, you may be required to cut and paste sections from your traditionally formatted résumé. During this process, you may lose the formatting. Do not worry. Visual appeal is not an issue for this process and formatting does not matter. You are merely dropping your information into a database. Your focus should be on utilizing key words and phrases that sell your skills and quantify your accomplishments.

The second consideration when converting a traditional résumé to an online version is sending it as an attachment while preserving formatting. If you are sending your résumé electronically as an attachment, it is best to send it either as a Microsoft (MS) Word file or as a portable document file (.pdf). Doing so ensures that the résumé layout is properly maintained through the file transfer. Sending your résumé as a .pdf file also ensures that those who do not use the same word processing software as you are able to read the file.

Most colleges and career centers now have electronic job boards that allow students to upload their résumés for recruiters and employers to view. There are also many niche job boards specific to industries. Another popular means of sharing an electronic résumé is through social media sites. Just be certain that you are posting your information on valid business sites and not personal sites. As with a traditional job search, keep track of and monitor all activity with your online search.

When posting your résumé online, always date your resume and update it every two to three months. Most employers won't view online résumés that are more than six months old. Guard your personal information by posting your résumé only on reputable job search sites. Just as with a hard-copy résumé, protect your identity and do not include personal information of any kind, including photographs, marital status, birth dates, or your Social Security number.

In some instances employers, will request that an **electronic formatted résumé** be submitted. Electronic formatted résumés are résumés that are submitted in American Standard Code for Information Interchange (ASCII) format. Once the employer receives your electronic formatted résumé, the résumé is added to a specialized database/software that routinely scans résumés based on key words (qualifications/skills) for specific jobs. The résumé is used to match key words contained in your résumé with specific jobs. Therefore, on this type of résumé, list as many key words as possible related to your target job. For electronic formatted résumés, visual appeal is not an issue. Electronic formatted résumés use Times New Roman font size 10 to 14. An electronic formatted résumé should be left-justified. Avoid tabs and centering. Headings should be in all capital letters. Hard returns must be used instead of word wrap. Avoid bold, italics, underlines, graphics, percent signs, and foreign characters. Also avoid boxes, horizontal and vertical lines, solid/hollow bullets, and table and column formatting.

Content for electronic formatted résumés include having your name at the top of the page on its own line. Standard address formatting (as when addressing a letter) should be used. Use key words specific to your desired job category and/or when communicating your knowledge, skills, and abilities. Work experience dates should have beginning and ending dates on the same line. Use asterisks or dashes (no bullets or boxes of any kind) and list each telephone number on its own line (no parentheses around area codes). Date your electronic résumé. Just as with hard-copy résumés, do not include personal information of any kind, including photographs, marital status, birth dates, or your Social Security number. See Figure 7 for an example of an electronic formatted résumé.

Electronic Résumé Example,
see Figure 7

Cover Letters

A **cover letter** is often the first impression a potential employer will have of you. It serves as an introduction to your résumé. Employers use cover letters as screening tools.

When writing a cover letter, use a friendly but professional tone. Use complete sentences and proper grammar. When tailoring your cover letter, include information about the target company that communicates to the employer you have conducted research on the company. In a cover letter, communicate how your key skills, experience, and accomplishments can meet the employer's needs. This is accomplished by identifying the skills and qualifications the target employer is requesting in the job announcement and/or job description and matching these needs with your key skills and qualifications. Let the employer know what you can offer the company, not what you want from the company. In the paragraph where you are communicating your key skills and experience, refer the reader to the attached résumé. Do not duplicate what is already listed on your résumé; instead, emphasize your experience and key skills. Although it is acceptable to utilize the words "I and my" in a cover letter, be careful to not begin most of your sentences with the word "I". Instead, focus the attention toward the employer. This puts the company first and makes its needs more important. Attempt to begin a sentence with what the company will receive with your skills. For example:

Instead of writing, "*I* am proficient in Word,"

Write, "*Your* company will benefit from my proficiency in Word."

Address the cover letter to a specific person. This should be the person who will be making the hiring decision. Do not address your cover letter to a department, the company name, or "to whom it may concern." Call the company and ask for a specific name and title, identifying the appropriate spelling and gender. If you have conducted research and still cannot secure a specific name, use a subject line instead of a salutation. For example, instead of writing, "To Whom It May Concern," write, "Subject: Account Clerk Position." If you have talked to a specific person at your target company, refer to the previous communication. Include the specific position you are seeking in your cover letter and how you learned about the job opening. At the end of your cover letter, request an interview (not the job). Do not write that you look forward to the employer contacting you. Display initiative by stating that you will follow up on your request for an interview within the next week. Include an enclosure notation for your résumé and close courteously.

Use the proper business-letter format for your cover letter. Each word and paragraph in your cover letter must have a purpose. Your goal is to communicate how your knowledge, skills, abilities, and accomplishments fill a targeted company's needs and make the reader want to review your résumé. The cover-letter setup in Figure 8 and sample cover letters in Figures 9 and 10 will help you create a winning cover letter.

Cover Letter Setup,
see Figure 8

Cover Letter Example 1,
see Figure 9

Cover Letter Example 2,
see Figure 10

Print your cover letter on the same type of paper used for your résumé. Copy the information heading you created for your résumé and use it on your cover letter. This creates a consistent and professional visual appeal for your résumé package. Avoid making common mistakes, including typographical or grammatical errors, forgetting to include a date, or forgetting to sign the cover letter. Complete and grammatically correct sentences must be used on a cover letter. As with your résumé, have someone you trust proofread your letter before you send it to a potential employer. Any error communicates a lack of attention to detail. Even minor errors have the potential to disqualify you from securing an interview.

Tailoring Your Résumé and Cover Letter

Tailored Package, see Figure 11

Tailor your résumé and cover letter specifically to each job and company for which you are applying. Carefully review the target job announcement. If possible, secure a copy of the job description from the company's human resource department if it is not available or attached to the job posting. Identify key job skills that the position requires, and highlight the company needs with your skills. As you learned in step four of creating your résumé, utilize the O*Net website to identify key skills for your targeted position. If necessary, rearrange the order of the information presented on your résumé so that the key skills required for your target position are presented first. On your cover letter, emphasize your specific qualifications that match those required for the open position. Figure 11 provides an example of a résumé and cover letter tailored to a specific job announcement.

Although mentioned earlier, it cannot be stressed enough that a daytime phone number and e-mail address need to be listed on both the cover letter and résumé. Because most invitations for job interviews occur over the phone, your phone voice-mail and/or message machine need to be professional. Do not include musical introductions or any other greeting that would not make a positive first impression to a potential employer. Maintain a professional e-mail address to use in your job search.

Cory's friend Rebecca was a practical joker. Cory enjoyed calling Rebecca because her voice-mail message started with a joke or had some strange voice and/or music. However, the last time Cory called Rebecca, Cory noticed that Rebecca's message was normal. The next time Cory saw Rebecca, Cory asked Rebecca why her voice message was suddenly so serious. Rebecca explained that she had recently applied for a job and had been selected to interview. However, she was embarrassed because when the interviewer called to arrange the appointment, the interviewer left a message and also suggested that Rebecca change her voice-mail message to a more professional message.

Tips for Ex-Offenders

If you have served time in prison and are now attempting to reenter the workforce, you are to be congratulated for wanting to move forward with your life. Others have made poor choices in their past, and you have made restitution for yours. Be honest with the potential employer.

On your résumé, include all jobs you have held and skills you learned while incarcerated. List the correctional facility in place of the employer for these jobs. List all education, including degrees and courses you received while incarcerated. Include the educational institution that provided the training.

The employment application is a legal document. At the bottom of this document, applicants sign a statement that affirms that all information provided on the application is true. Therefore, you must not lie. If, after being hired, your employer discovers that you have lied on the application, you may be immediately terminated. The majority of applications ask if you have been convicted of a felony. Please note that arrests are not convictions. If you have been convicted of a felony, check "Yes." The application should also have a space to write a statement after the felony question. Do not leave this space blank. In this space, write, "Will explain in detail during interview."

Workplace Dos and Don'ts

Do keep your résumé updated with skills and accomplishments	*Don't* wait until the last minute to update your résumé
Do change your résumé format after you have gained work experience	*Don't* use outdated reference names and letters
Do use the correct format for your résumé	*Don't* send out a résumé or cover letter that has not been proofread by someone you can trust
Do check your résumé and cover letter for errors before sending them to employers	*Don't* forget to sign your cover letter

YOUR NAME (16 point, bold)
Your Address (12 or 14 point, bold)
City, State ZIP
Phone Number (Include Area Code)
E-Mail Address (Remove Hyperlink)

Horizontal line optional and thickness varies

OBJECTIVE Headings can be on the left or centered, 12- or 14-point font, and uppercase or initial cap.
Format headings the same throughout the resumé.
Keep spacing equal between each section.

QUALIFICATIONS (OR SKILLS)
- Relate to target job, all job-related skills and transferable skills
- Most relative to the job are listed first
- Bullet (small round or small square only) these items to stand out

> Emphasize skills and education. List your skills and education before any work experience.

EDUCATION
You may list before qualifications
Do not list high school if you have graduated from college
Include the dates and align to the right
List schools in chronological order, most recent attended first

WORK EXPERIENCE
Include: *Name of Company* and City, State—No Addresses
Job title bolded, if part-time, dates employed (month, year)
List the jobs in chronological order, most recent first align dates to the right
Align dates to the right
List the duties, responsibilities, and achievements
Be consistent in your setup
Use the same tense throughout (*ed* or *ing*)
Do not use complete sentences or *I, me,* or *my*

OTHER CAPABILITIES
Optional items in this section may not be directly related to the job but may interest the employer such as honors or awards.

> **Keep in mind**
> - Watch periods, punctuation
> - Watch spelling
> - Use a regular font, no color, 12-point font (except heading)
> - Use resumé paper, no dark or bright colors
> - Do not use full sentences or *I, me,* or *my*
> - References are not necessary; you will have a separate sheet with references
> - Do not use graphics

Figure 1

Functional Résumé Layout

Suzie S. Kringle
1234 Tolearn Avenue, Meadeville, PA 16335
555-555-5555
skringle05@careerssuccess.lns

OBJECTIVE

To obtain a position as a Junior Accountant with Owen Company where I can utilize my general accounting skills in a dynamic company.

SKILLS

- Knowledgeable and accurate in general ledger and journal posting
- Basic software knowledge of QuickBooks
- Knowledge of account receivables and account payables
- Experienced with Microsoft Office, including Word, Excel, Access, PowerPoint, and Outlook
- Ten-key at 150 cspm
- Type 50 wpm accurately
- Excellent English grammar, spelling, and punctuation skills
- Accurately follow oral and written instructions
- Strong attention to detail
- Positive attitude, motivated, and organized

EDUCATION

State University, Meadeville, PA   5/12
Bachelor of Science Degree in Business, Accounting

Meadeville City College, Meadeville PA   5/10
Associate in Arts Degree in Business, Certificate of Completion in Account Clerk Program

WORK EXPERIENCE

S and L Accounting   Edinboro, PA   1/10–present
Account Clerk
Assist the Accountant by answering telephone, bookkeeping, data entry in Excel and QuickBooks, verifying totals, making copies, faxing, and other clerical duties when needed.

Bret's Hamburger Haven   Edinboro, PA   1/07–12/09
Cashier/Food Service
Worked as a team member to assist customers with food orders, cleaned, handled cash, and trained new employees.

Figure 2

Functional Résumé Example
with Minimal Career Work
Experience

HEIDI H. KRINGLE

1234 Tolearn Avenue, Meadeville, PA 16335
555-555-5555   hkringle02@careersuccess.lns

OBJECTIVE

To obtain a position as an Office Assistant with Austin Office Supplies that will enable me to utilize my current skills and education.

QUALIFICATIONS

- Type 50 wpm
- Experienced with Microsoft Office, including Word, Excel, Access, PowerPoint, and Outlook
- Accurately proofread and edit documents
- Knowledge of records management
- Positive telephone skills
- Excellent oral and written communications skills
- Positive attitude, motivated, and organized
- Excellent customer services skills

EDUCATION/CERTIFICATION

2010–2012   Meadeville City College   Meadeville, PA
Associate of Art Degree, Business & Technology
Clerical Administration Certificate
GPA 3.9, Dean's list

EXPERIENCE

06/2009–present   Fine Linens by Jen   Meadeville, PA
Cashier
Responsibilities include: providing customer service, cashiering, placing merchandise on the floor, helping return go backs, processing merchandise on the floor, stocking merchandise in back/stockroom, training new hires.

02/2003–05/2009   Jerry's Burger Place   Meadeville, PA
Cashier/Counter Person
Responsibilities included: assisted guests with their orders, ensured a safe and clean work environment, and assisted other team members as needed.

Figure 3

Functional Résumé
Example without Career
Work Experience

YOUR NAME (16 point, bold)

Your Address (12 or 14 point, bold) ■ **City, State ZIP** ■ **Phone Number** (Include Area Code)
E-Mail Address (Remove Hyperlink)

PERSONAL PROFILE:

Include key skill sets. Headings can be on the left or centered, 12- or 14-point font, and uppercase or initial cap. Format headings the same throughout the resumé.
Keep the spacing equal between each section.

PROFESSIONAL EXPERIENCE:

Group key skills, experience, and accomplishments under each major skill set heading.

First Skill Set Subheading

- Communicate experience, and key accomplishments relating to your first skill set subheading
- Using power words, quantify as much as possible
- Include duties, responsibilities, and achievements

> Emphasize key skill sets and accomplishments. List work experience before education and employment history.

Second Skill Set Subheading

- Relate statements to target job. Communicate both job-related skills or transferable skills
- Accomplishments and experience most relative to target job are listed first
- Bullet (small round or small square only) accomplishments and experience to stand out

Third Skill Set Subheading

- Be consistent in setup
- Use same tense throughout (ed or ing)
- Do not use complete sentences or I, me, or my

> **Keep in mind**
>
> - Watch punctuation, and spelling
> - Can be one or two pages. If two pages, place name on second page
> - Use a regular font, no color, 12-point font (except heading)
> - Do not use full sentences or *I, me,* or *my*
> - Do not use graphics
> - Align bullets to the right

WORK HISTORY:

Name of Company and City, State—No Addresses—dates employed (month, year)
Job title (bold title, NOT employer)
List jobs in chronological order with most recent date first

EDUCATION:

Do not list high school
Include the years attended, areas of study, and degrees earned
List schools in chronological order, most recent attended first

PROFESSIONAL AFFILIATIONS/CERTIFICATIONS:

List professional memberships including the name of the organization, status (member, board member, etc.) and dates of membership. Also include any certifications or community service activities that are relevant to the target job.

Figure 4

Chronological
Résumé Layout

PEARL B. KRINGLE, CPA

1234 Tolearn Avenue ▲ Meadeville, PA 16335 ▲ 555.555.5555
pbkringle@careerssuccess.lns

PROFILE:

Highly experienced, personable, and detail-oriented Certified Public Accountant with expertise and demonstrated leadership in the areas of accounting, computer information systems, and quantitative analysis.

PROFESSIONAL EXPERIENCE:

Accounting

- Audit cash, investments, payables, fixed assets, and prepaid expenses for small business enterprises, corporations, and not-for-profit organizations.
- Collect and analyze data to detect deficient controls, extravagance, fraud, or non-compliance with laws, regulations, and management policies.
- Prepare detailed reports on audit findings, report to management about asset utilization and audit results, and recommend changes in operations and financial activities.
- Inspect account books and accounting systems for efficiency, effectiveness, and use of accepted accounting procedures to record transactions.
- Examine and evaluate financial and information systems, recommending controls to ensure system reliability and data integrity.
- Confer with company officials about financial and regulatory matters.

Computer Information Systems

- Developed information resources, providing data security/control, strategic computing, and disaster recovery.
- Consulted with users, management, vendors, and technicians to assess computing needs and system requirements.
- Stayed abreast of advances in technology and forwarded research and recommendations to ensure company and respective clients were utilizing proper and most efficient tools and information systems.
- Met with department heads, managers, supervisors, vendors to solicit cooperation and resolve problems.
- Provided users with technical support for computer problems.

Quantitative Analysis

- Assembled computerized spreadsheets, draw charts, and graphs used to illustrate technical reports.
- Analyzed financial information to produce forecasts of business, industry, and economic conditions for use in making investment decisions.
- Maintained knowledge and stayed abreast of developments in the fields of industrial technology, business, finance, and economic theory.
- Interpreted data affecting investment programs, such as price, yield, stability, future trends in investment risks, and economic influences.

Figure 6

Chronological Résumé
Example with Degree

PEARL B. KRINGLE, CPA

Page Two

- Monitored fundamental economic, industrial, and corporate developments through the analysis of information obtained from financial publications and services, investment banking firms, government agencies, trade publications, company sources, and personal interviews.
- Recommended investments and investment timing to companies, investment firm staff, or the investing public.
- Determined the prices at which securities should be syndicated and offered to the public.
- Prepared plans of action for investment based on financial analyses.

WORK HISTORY:

Coopers & Lion, LLP, Alltown, PA *Auditor*	May 2010–present
Mitchell Ho, CPA, Atlanta, GA *General Accountant*	May 2007–April 2010
U.S. Department of Labor, Atlanta, GA *Program Assistant*	January 2005–February 2007
Grace's Burger Palace, Riverside, GA *Server*	August 2001–December 2004

EDUCATION AND LICENSE:

Masters of Computer Information Systems Georgia State University, Atlanta, GA	August 2012
Certified Public Accountant – State of Georgia	May 2010
Bachelor of Science in Accounting Heather Glenn College, Heather Glenn, NC	May 2007

PROFESSIONAL AFFILIATIONS:

American Institute of Certified Financial Accountants
Beta Alpha Psi Fraternity
National Association of Black Accountants

Figure 5

Chronological Resumé
Example with Degree page 2
(*continued*)

Steven Mark Kringle

1234 Tolearn Avenue ■ Meadeville, PA 16335 ■ 555.555.5555
smkringle@careersuccess.lns

PERSONAL PROFILE

Results and efficiency focused professional with experience in sales/vendor relations, inventory/ warehousing, and management/supervision. Proven ability in relationship management with demonstrated and consistent increase in sales over a five-year period. Inventory expertise includes streamlined operations, improved productivity, and favorable inventory ratio utilization for wholesale food supplier. Management ability to create goal-driven teams, groom leaders, and facilitate the creation of a learning organization.

PROFESSIONAL EXPERIENCE

Customer Service Orientation ■ Innovative Risk Taker ■ Excellent Quantitative Skills ■ Purchasing, Inventory Planning & Control ■ Supply Chain Management ■ Warehouse Operations ■ Process Improvement ■ Cost Containment ■ Hiring, Staffing & Scheduling Safety Training ■ Excellent Computer Knowledge

Sales/Vendor Relations

- Through the establishment of vendor relationships, schedule product installations, exchanges, buy-backs or removals of equipment or other assets including supplier networks and agent contacts in order to meet customer expectations for private soda company. Have grown sales territory from two county area to tri-state contract area over four-year period.

- Source and facilitate delivery of product (e.g., beverage equipment, parts, point of sale material, return of assets) for retail suppliers. Sales complaints are consistently .05% per year, while sales volume and customer satisfaction rates are the highest of all sales team and consistently grow.

- Research and resolve issues for customers, business partners, and Company associates in order to expedite service, installations, or orders using information systems and working with supply chain partners.

- Create and maintain partnerships with customers, clients or third party service providers (e.g., contract service/installation agents, distributors) by establishing common goals, objectives, and performance target requirements in order to improve customer service and satisfaction.

- Created troubleshooting equipment process which allows retail suppliers to receive immediate response on service issues (e.g., beverage vending, dispensing) via telephone or Internet to minimize customer down time and service cost.

Figure 6

Chronological Résumé
Example with No Degree

Steven Mark Kringle

Page Two

Inventory/Warehousing

- Responsible for maintaining customer contact to confirm service or orders including accuracy, service follow up, equipment service confirmation, product delivery confirmation, and routine service scheduling for local foodservice broker.

- Received, recorded, and responded to customer or consumer inquiries/feedback using specially designed database which documented best practices from nationwide foodservice association in an effort to provide improved service, order accuracy, and optimized supply chain efficiency. Information was collected, analyzed, and reported to all members of the supply chain for feedback and control purposes.

- Processed orders for goods and services with food service business partners, customers, suppliers, and company associates, either through direct telephone contact or electronic means, to increase speed and accuracy of order transactions and improve loss prevention systems.

Management/Supervision

- Developed and trained team members on inventory control, customer service, and safety for local foodservice provider. Program was so successful customers within the company supply chain requested and received training. To date, over 500 individuals have received custom training.

- Supervised cross-functional team of 100 including order technicians, outside repair personnel, transportation associates, warehouse attendants, and loss prevention specialists.

- As assistant-manager for college-town restaurant, assisted in the hiring, training, scheduling, and performance evaluation of staff for small soda company and local food service supplier.

WORK HISTORY

Christopher Cola Company, Susanville, NE   2007–2012
Vendor Relations Associate

Joshua Food Service, Pocatoe, NE   2005–2007
Warehouse Manager

Nick-Mike Ribs 'N Stuff, Pocatoe, NE   2003–2005
Assistant Restaurant Manager

EDUCATION/PROFESSIONAL DEVELOPMENT

University of Nebraska, Lincoln, NE   2009–2012
Business Management/Marketing

Figure 6

Chronological Résumé
Example with No Degree
(*continued*)

AUTUMN S. KRINGLE
1234 TOLEARN AVENUE,
MEADEVILLE, PA 16335
555-555-5555
askringle@careersuccess.lns

OBJECTIVE

Bookkeeper

KEY WORD SUMMARY

Bookkeeping skills, financial management, accounting, receivables and payroll, organized, data entry, communication skills, problem solving, responsible, team player, computer skills.

EDUCATION

City College: City, WA
2012
Associate Degree in Accounting

COURSES OF STUDY
----

* Intro to Accounting
* Intro to Business
* MS Office
* Workplace Communication
* Office Accounting
* Business Law
* Intro to Marketing

COMPUTER SKILLS
----

* Microsoft Office: Word, Excel, Access, PowerPoint
* WordPerfect
* Internet

WORK EXPERIENCE

Yang Enterprises: Fresno, CA
2010 – Present
Bookkeeping Assistant: Responsible for assisting accounting department with payroll, budgets, planning, and forecasting, purchasing, and managing accounts.

Figure 7

Electronic Resumé Example

Date of Letter

Employer's Name, Title
Company Name
Address
City, State Zip

Dear Mr./Ms./Dr.:

First Paragraph. Give the reason for the letter, the position for which you are applying, and how you learned of this position. Note any previous contact you may have had with the employer.

Second Paragraph. Tell why you are interested in the position, the organization, and its products or services. Indicate any research you have done on the position and/or the employer.

Third Paragraph. Refer to the attached resumé and highlight relevant aspects of your resumé. Emphasize the skills mentioned in the advertisement or on the job description. Provide specific reasons why the organization should hire you and what you can do to contribute to the organization's success.

Last Paragraph. Indicate your desire for an interview, and offer flexibility as to the time and place. Thank the employer for his or her consideration and express anticipation in meeting him or her. Include a phone number and e-mail address for contact.

Sincerely,

(Do not forget to sign your cover letter)

Your Name
Your Address
City, State Zip

Enclosure

Figure 8

Cover Letter Setup

September 25, 2015

Owen Corporation
Attention Brandon Owen
435 East Chesny Street
Meadeville, PA 16335

Dear Mr. Owen:

As a recent accounting graduate of State University, Meadeville, I was delighted to learn from your web site of the available Junior Accountant position. The purpose of this letter is to express a strong interest in becoming an Owen Company Accountant at your Meadeville facility. In addition to possessing a B.S. degree in Business, Accounting, I am responsible and consider myself a leader.

Owen Company sponsors a variety of community services and employee recognition programs, which I have read a great deal about. Your company has earned my respect, as it has from much of the community for your involvement in the after-school programs in Meadeville Unified School District.

As you will see on the attached resumé, Owen Company would benefit from the skills I have learned throughout college. These include: general ledger and journal posting; Microsoft Word, Excel, and Access programs; Quickbooks; and accurate ten-key (150 cspm). In addition, I also offer a superior work ethic, strong communicative abilities, attention to detail, and a keen interest in upgrading my skills.

I am confident that my skills and abilities will make me an ideal candidate for a position in this field. I would appreciate an opportunity to meet with you to discuss how my skills can meet the needs of Owen Company. I will contact you by phone within the week to discuss the possibility of an interview.

Sincerely,

Suzie Kringle

Suzie Kringle
1234 Tolearn Avenue
Meadeville, PA 16335

Enclosure

Figure 9

Cover Letter Example 1

HEIDI H. KRINGLE

1234 Tolearn Avenue, Meadeville, PA 16335
555-555-5555   hshore02@careersuccess.lns

September 21, 2015

Mr. Jared Bill
Austin Office Supplies
1122 Friendly Road
Meadeville, PA 93725

Dear Mr. Bill:

I recently spoke with Gene Armstrong, an employee at your company, and he recommended that I send you a copy of my resumé. Knowing the requirements for the position and that I am interested in working at this type of establishment, he felt that I would be an ideal candidate for your office assistant position.

My personal goal is to be a part of an organization such as yours that wants to excel in both growth and profit. I would welcome the opportunity to be employed at Austin's Office Supplies since this is the largest and best-known office supply company in the city. Your company has a reputation of excellent products and service.

Austin's Office Supplies would benefit from someone such as I who is accustomed to a fast-paced environment where deadlines are a priority and handling multiple jobs simultaneously is the norm. As you can see on the attached resumé, my previous jobs required me to be well organized, accurate, and friendly. I enjoy a challenge and work hard to attain my goals. Great customer skills are important in a business such as yours.

Nothing would please me more than to be a part of your team. I would like very much to discuss with you how I could contribute to your organization with my office skills and my dependability. I will contact you next week to arrange an interview. In the interim, I can be reached at 555-555-5555.

Sincerely,

Heidi H. Kringle

Heidi H. Kringle

Enclosure

Figure 10

Cover Letter Example 2

ACCOUNT CLERK – position #022394   full time, permanent posit

The current vacancy is a full-time position at Viau Technical College.

Definition: Under direction performs a wide variety of entry-level accounting/busines office work.

Compensation: Starts at $3,176 per month. Full-time permanent positions provide an attractive benefit package which include health, dental, and vision coverage for the employee and eligible dependents, as well as life insurance and disability coverage for employees.

Experience: Entry-level experience performing general accounting duties.

Education: Formal or informal education equivalent to completion of an Associate Degree in accounting.

Examples of Duties: Performs a wide variety of duties including but not limited to: basic accounting work; verifying, balancing, and posting/recording accounting informatic verifying and preparing invoices, checks, correspondence, and statistical information; proof-reading; and filing. Calculates, prepares, and reconciles various financial reports. Entering and retrieving data from computer system as needed. Assigning and/or reviewi the work of other employees and students. May perform other related duties as needed.

Required Knowledge and Abilities:
Knowledge of sequence of procedures in the accounting cycle, analysis, use, and interpretation of accounting and financial data; and modern office practices. Knowledge of and ability to employ proper English usage, spelling, grammar, and punctuation. Skil make deposits, process checks, and reconcile accounts; employ mathematical and statistic techniques sufficient to maintain district records; keyboard; utilize word processing software, email, online calendaring, and data entry/retrieval from database programs; and create and utilize spreadsheets. Ability to assign, monitor, and/or review the work of others; receive and follow instructions and appropriately interact with students, staff, faculty, and the public; and learn and apply college and district policies and procedures.

Selection Process: The selection process will include screening to ensure application are complete and meet all minimum qualifications. This process will also include a written test of knowledge and abilities (35% weight), a performance test (35% weight), a an oral appraisal board interview (30% weight). Of those candidates achieving a passi score on the first test, only the 30 highest scoring candidates, plus ties, will be invited the performance exam. Of those candidates achieving a passing score on the performar exam, only the 15 highest scoring candidates, plus ties, will be invited to the oral appraisal board interview. Passing score is 75% out of 100% on each testing section.

FIRST EXAM IS TENTATIVELY SCHEDULED FOR SATURDAY, JUNE 20, 2015.

To move forward in the selection process, you must complete an online application through our web site at www.viaucommunitycollege.com. Resumes may also be submitted by mail, in person, or by emailing to job@viaucommunitycollege.com.

Filing Deadline: 4:30 p.m., Monday, June 1, 2015.

Figure 11

Tailored Package—Page 1
Job Announcement

Jolene M. Kringle

1234 Tolearn Avenue ■ Meadville, PA ■ 555.555.5555
jmkringle@careersuccess.lns

Objective

Highly motivated, responsible, and ethical individual seeks an entry-level accounting position with Viau Technical College in an effort to apply newly acquired general business and accounting skills. Experienced in basic accounting procedures, operational efficiencies, and logistics.

Key Skills & Qualifications

- Strong math and analytical skills
- Data entry
- Bilingual (Spanish–speak and write)
- Works well in group environments
- Excellent grammatical and English usage
- Proficient in MAS 90 and Quickbooks

- Demonstrate leadership
- Maintain records and filing
- Strong attention to detail
- Experience with balancing and posting
- Accurately proofread and edit documents
- Proficient in Word, Excel, Access, Outlook

Education

Hill Valley Technical College, Clarkville, PA   01/10–06/12
Associate of Arts Degree, Accounting

Work Experience

El Montes Restaurant, Reedville, PA   12/08–present
Bookkeeper/Server
Perform bookkeeping functions for small family business including creation and analysis of financial statements, cash/banking functions, and communication with CPA firm. Implemented electronic accounting and inventory system which saved the company an estimated $50K. Serve as Lead Server for evening staff. In addition to exemplary customer service and cashier duties, responsibilities include inventory control, and training of new staff training in both customer service and food safety/handling for busy Mexican food restaurant.

Freshwide Marketing, Lewis, PA   05–09/08, 09, 10
Quality Control Clerk (*seasonal*)
Received and counted stock items and recorded data. Monitored fruit and produce as it arrived or was shipped from cold storage for twenty independent fruit growers. Verified inventory computations by comparing them to physical counts of stock, and investigated discrepancies or adjusted errors. Stored items in an orderly and accessible manner in cold storage and warehouse.

Starlight Produce, Lewis, PA   06/06–09/08
Shipping Manifest Clerk
As a shipping clerk for regional fruit packer, prepared, monitored, and facilitated orders for shipping to over fifty clients throughout the United States. Duties included examining contents and comparing with records, such as manifests, invoices, or orders, to verify accuracy of incoming or outgoing shipment. Prepared documents, such as work orders, bills of lading, and shipping orders to route materials. Determined shipping method for materials, using knowledge of shipping procedures, routes, and rates.

Figure 11

Tailored Package—Page 2
Resumé (*continued*)

Jolene M. Kringle

1234 Tolearn Avenue ■ Meadeville, PA 16335 ■ 555.555.5555

jmkringle@careersuccess.lns

April 21, 2015

Monique Marshall, Director
Human Resource Department
Viau Community College
60157 S. Holbrook
Viau, PA 12150

RE: Account Clerk Position #022394

Dear Ms. Marshall:

It is with great excitement that I am submitting the following application package
for consideration of your current full time Account Clerk Position posted on the Viau
Community College web site. Viau Community College has a legacy of quality and
excellence in education and nothing would please me more than to apply my newly
acquired accounting education to your organization.

As you can see on the attached resumé, your company will benefit from my demonstrated
leadership in the areas of general accounting, business, and computer applications.
Excelling in the creation and quantitative analysis of basic financial statements, I am familiar
with both the installation and utilization of common accounting software programs. At my
current job, interaction with both the company owners and the company's contracted CPA
firm is a weekly required activity which has greatly improved my communication and
presentation skills. In my opinion, diversity is a valuable asset and I enjoy utilizing my
fluency in speaking Spanish when interacting with customers. I consider myself an ethical
and responsible individual with excellent verbal and written communication skills.

It would be a privilege to have the opportunity to discuss how my knowledge, skills, and
professional experience can contribute to the continued success of the Viau Community
College. I will contact you within the next week to follow-up on my application materials.
In the interim, I can be reached at 555-555-5555 or via e-mail at jmkringle@careersuccess.lns.

Sincerely,

Jolene M. Kringle

Jolene M. Kringle

Enclosures

Figure 11

Tailored Package—Page 3
Cover Letter (*continued*)

Jolene M. Kringle

1234 Tolearn Avenue ■ Meadeville, PA 16335 ■ 555.555.5555

jmkringle@careersuccess.lns

Professional Reference List

Name	Relationship	Phone	E-mail	Mailing Address
Autumn Hart	Former Accounting Instructor, Hill Valley Technical College	555.555-1111	atmnhrt@hillvalley.scl	123 Hillvalley Clarkville, PA
Gloria Montes	Owner, El Montes Restaurant	555.555-1112	gloria@eatelmontes.fat	5432 Food Ct. Reedville, PA
Gary Solis	Floor Manager, Freshwide Marketing	555.555-1113	solisg@freshwide.fruit	2220 Tulare Lewis, PA
Patty Negoro	Office Manager, Starlight Produce	555.555-1114	pattyn@starlight.sun	444 Adoline Lewis, PA

Figure 11

Tailored Package—Page 4
Reference List (*continued*)

Concept Review and Application

Summary of Key Concepts

- A winning résumé makes it easy for potential employers to quickly and easily identify your skills and experience
- Update your résumé with new skills and accomplishments at least once a year
- Include both job-specific skills and transferable skills on your résumé
- Use the correct résumé layout for your career work experience
- A cover letter is most often an employer's first impression of you
- Check that your résumé and cover letter are free of typographical and grammatical errors
- Share your résumé electronically as a .pdf file to ensure the résumé layout is maintained

Key Terms

chronological résumé

functional résumé

  layout

résumé

cover letter

information heading

job-specific skills

soft skills

electronic formatted

  résumé

power words

transferable skills

If You Were the Boss

1. What would you look for first when reviewing a résumé?
2. What would your reaction be if you were reading a cover letter that had several typing and grammar errors?

Video Case Study: Résumé and Cover Letter Tips

Pearson Education

This video presents expert advice on how to write a winning résumé and cover letter. To view these videos, visit the Student Resources: Professionalism section in www.mystudentsuccesslab.com. Then answer the following questions.

1. Share four common résumé mistakes and solutions.
2. Explain how to utilize a job announcement when preparing a résumé and cover letter.
3. Share four common cover-letter mistakes and solutions.
4. What information should be repeated in a cover letter that is already included on a résumé?

Web Links

www.onetcenter.org/

http://resume.monster.com

http://jobstar.org/tools/resume/index.htm

http://jobsearch.about.com/od/networking

Activities

Activity 1

Conduct an Internet search to identify five new power words to include in your résumé.

1. _____

2. _____

3. _____

4. _____

5. _____

Activity 2

Search for a job you would like to have when you graduate, and fill in the following information that will be used to tailor your résumé and create a cover letter.

Position for which you are applying	
How you learned about the job	
Any contact you have had with the employer or others about the job	
Why are you interested in this job?	
Why are you interested in this company?	
What products or services are provided?	
List relevant skills related to the job description	
List reasons this company should hire you	
Indicate your desire for an interview	
Indicate your flexibility for an interview (time and place)	

Activity 3

Using a word-processing program and the steps and/or exercises from this chapter, create a résumé for the job you found in Activity 2.

Activity 4

Using a word processing program and the information from this chapter, create a cover letter for the job you found in Activity 2.

Activity 5

Change the résumé from activity 3 to an electronic formatted résumé.

Sample Exam Questions

1. Update your résumé at least _____.

2. If you are starting a new career, create a résumé using the _____.

3. A/An _____ résumé format emphasizes your related work experience and skills.

4. _____ skills are those that are directly related to a specific job.

5. _____ skills are transferable from one job to the next.

6. Use _____ words whenever possible in your résumé; they describe your accomplishments in a lively and specific way.

7. The _____ is an introduction to your résumé.

Suggested Readings

Schuller, N. M., Ickes, L., and Schullery, S. E. "Employer Preferences for Resumes and Cover Letters," *Business Communication Quarterly* 72 (June 2009): 163–176.

"2010 Resume: What's In, What's Out," *Administrative Professional Today* 36 (March 2010): 1–2.

Schaffer, G. "Six Ways to Ruin Your Resume," *Computerworld* 43 (April 13, 2009): 26–28.

Job Search Skills

Job Search Skills

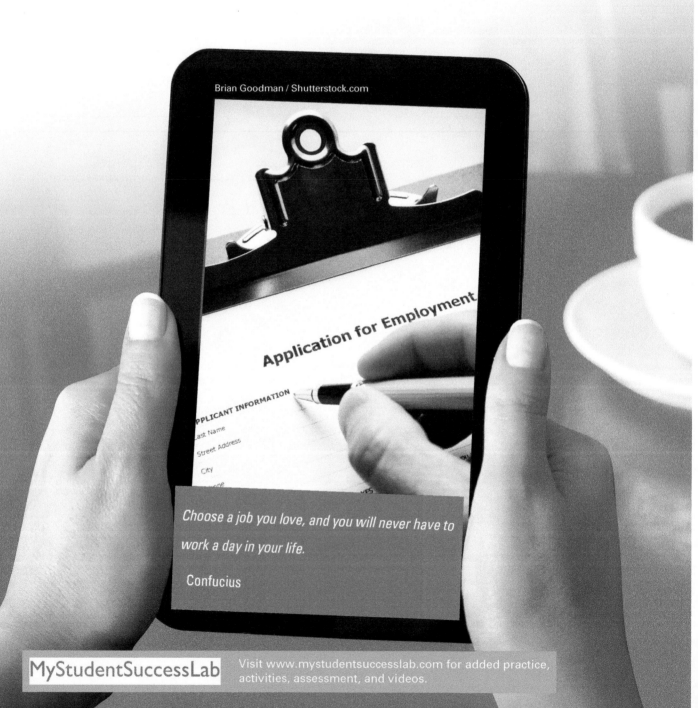

Brian Goodman / Shutterstock.com

Application for Employment

APPLICANT INFORMATION
Last Name
Street Address
City

Choose a job you love, and you will never have to work a day in your life.

Confucius

MyStudentSuccessLab   Visit www.mystudentsuccesslab.com for added practice, activities, assessment, and videos.

How-Do-You-Rate

	Are you job search savvy?	True	False
1.	It is best to attend a job fair alone.	❏	❏
2.	It is acceptable to distribute personal business cards at social functions.	❏	❏
3.	It is not necessary to share personal information such as a birthdate and Social Security number during a job search.	❏	❏
4.	A job search portfolio is a foundation for the interview portfolio.	❏	❏
5.	Most realistic job leads are found through informal networks.	❏	❏

Objectives

- Utilize the *self-discovery* process to identify the right career
- Conduct a *targeted job search,* including a realistic job preview
- Determine the *cost of living* in your desired work location
- Ensure a professional *electronic image*
- Create a *job search portfolio*
- Identify references to be used in your job search
- Identify sources for job leads
- Demonstrate appropriate behaviors for the application process
- Define *networking* and create a professional *network*

If you answered "true" to three or more of these questions, congratulations—you are well on your way to finding the job of your dreams. Knowing how the job search process works, creating a job search plan, and properly utilizing job search tools pave the way to job search success.

The Job Search

An effective job search is the key to finding a great job. A successful job search involves creating a plan, conducting research, and taking action. Doing so takes time, organization, communication, and professionalism (all key skills you have developed throughout this text). This chapter is designed to help you create a job search strategy. A successful job search strategy identifies what type of job you will be looking for, what tools and resources you will need, and how these tools and resources are best used. The ultimate goal of a job search is to secure an interview that paves the way toward obtaining the job of your dreams.

Choosing the Right Career

Creating a job search plan begins with choosing the right career. This involves **self-discovery.** Self-discovery is the process of identifying key interests and skills built upon the career goals you set. Knowing your key selling points and linking these with your career goals will assist you in landing a job you will enjoy. The process of a career self-discovery includes identifying key interests and accomplishments from your work, educational, and personal experiences. A method for identifying key interests is creating an accomplishments worksheet. This is done by inventorying skills you have acquired from either your work or nonwork experience. Education and nonwork experience such as volunteerism are career-building experiences. The following trigger words assist you in identifying accomplishments:

Trigger Words

Adapted	Developed	Organized
Addressed	Earned	Planned
Analyzed	Established	Projected
Arranged	Financed	Recommended
Assisted	Implemented	Risked
Built	Increased	Saved
Calculated	Instructed	Staffed
Chaired	Installed	Taught
Cleaned	Introduced	Typed
Coached	Investigated	Updated
Communicated	Learned	Won
Coordinated	Located	Wrote
Created	Managed	
Determined	Motivated	

Exercise 1   Complete the Following Accomplishments Worksheet

Prior to answering each question, review the trigger words. Whenever possible, quantify your answers by documenting how many, how often, and how much. Do not worry if you cannot answer every question. The purpose of this exercise is to begin identifying accomplishments.

Question	Your Response (Quantify Your Answers)
1. What have you done in your career or career-building activities that you are most proud of?	
2. List something that you have achieved at work or school.	
3. What tasks have you performed at work and in career-building activities?	
4. What results have you produced from the tasks performed?	
5. List three things that demonstrate your ability to produce results.	
6. What have you done that shows an ability to successfully work with people?	
7. What else have you accomplished professionally or educationally that makes you proud?	
8. What extracurricular activities have you been involved with?	
9. List special skills or foreign languages you speak or write.	
10. What areas of interest do you have?	

Your accomplishments will be used to identify the right career, and they will also provide an excellent foundation when you begin to build your résumé.

After you have completed your accomplishments worksheet, reread your responses. They will most likely reveal a targeted career of interest to you.

A second means of identifying key skills and jobs of interest is to take a career assessment. Common career assessment tools include the Golden Personality Type Indicator, the Myers-Briggs Type Indicator, and the Strong Interest Inventory. Many college career centers offer these assessments, as do various online sources.

Conducting a realistic job preview identifies day-to-day and common tasks that are performed and required for a specific job. This common human resource management practice is used on job finalists prior to a job offer to ensure the candidate is fully aware of both the positive and negative aspects of a specific job. Be proactive and conduct your own realistic job preview. Identify any additional education or other requirements. For example, if you are a felon, you may not work in some areas of health care and education. There are other careers that require a clean DMV or credit history. Thoughtfully researching and understanding what is required to secure and succeed in a desired job early in the career exploration process will save time and money if the wrong career is selected.

Talk It Out

Review your completed accomplishments worksheet. What career area do you believe suits your skills and previous experiences?

Career Objective and Personal Profile

A foundation for both your job search strategy and building a winning résumé is to write a career objective or personal profile. A **career objective** is an introductory written statement for individuals with little or no work experience. A **personal profile** is an introductory written statement for individuals with professional experience related to their target career. These statements are used on a résumé to relate to the target career and/or employer, briefly introduce key skills, and express interest in a position. The responses from your completed accomplishments worksheet and career assessment provide a good summary of your current career goal based upon the knowledge, skills, and abilities you possess. Use this information as a foundation to create a statement that briefly and professionally describes you and your career goals. Depending on the layout of your résumé, this information will either have the heading "Career Objective" or "Personal Profile." This statement will be the first item listed on your résumé.

Web Quiz

Take the Career Planner Quiz to get a snapshot of your target job or find another career website.

http://careerpath.com/career-tests/?lr=cbmsn&siteid=cbmsnchcpath

As mentioned earlier, a career objective is an introductory written statement for individuals with little or no work experience. This is a brief statement that will include your interest in a specific position, a brief one-line description of your skills related to the position, and how your skills can benefit your target employer. The career objective is the only place on a résumé where it is acceptable to use the words "I" and "my."

Examples of Career Objectives

Objective: Seeking a position with an established accounting firm where I can utilize and apply my current accounting and computerized skills toward the excellence of Bell Company.

Objective: To obtain an Account Clerk position at Bell Company, where I can demonstrate and increase my general accounting skills to contribute to the success of the company.

Those with extensive work experience will utilize a personal profile. In creating a personal profile, review your key skills and accomplishments and group these items into general categories. Also identify key qualities you possess that are required for your target job. Take this information and turn it into a two- to three-sentence statement that provides a snapshot of your professional qualifications in a manner that sells your knowledge, skills, and abilities.

An Example of a Personal Profile

Personal Profile: Highly professional and detail-oriented accounting professional with demonstrated leadership and success in the areas of payroll, collections, and project management. Excellent analytical, communication, computer, and organizational skills. Bilingual (English/ Spanish).

Industry Research

One step toward a successful job search is research. When a job fits your personality and skills, you will more likely succeed. A satisfying career comes from working at a company that reflects your values and performing a job you enjoy. In chapter "Attitude, Goal Setting, and Life Management," you created goals for your career and personal life. Conducting industry research will reinforce that you have made the right career decision to support your life plan. In order to determine what type of industry you will research, identify industries that require your key skills. You may realize there is more potential for jobs that require your key skills than you thought.

Once you have identified industries requiring your skills, begin identifying specific jobs in these industries. Note the different job opportunities that exist within each industry. In addition, look at various job titles. Being aware of the various job titles you qualify for allows you more flexibility when job searching. After determining industries and job titles that fit your skills, identify the environments available, including where the jobs are located and specifically what type of work environment you desire.

For example, if you finished college with a business degree, you begin by conducting industry research on the skills you have acquired. Many different industries need employees with a business background, such as health care, educational institutions, and manufacturing. Once you have determined which industry or industries you would like to work for, you can begin reviewing job titles that fit the skills you have acquired in college, such as financial analyst, general accountant, marketing assistant, or human resource generalist. After identifying specific job titles that match your skill sets, decide what type of work environment you desire. If you select health care, you may have the choice of working in a hospital, a clinic, or a private physician's office.

Conducting industry and work environment research will provide you information that will make your job search easier and more successful. Instead of sending out hundreds of résumés in hopes of securing just any job, target companies that are a good match with your life plan, your skills, and your desired work environment.

The Targeted Job Search

After you have a clearly defined career objective and have identified jobs that suit your personal and career goals, it is time to begin a targeted job search. A **targeted job search** leads you through the process of discovering open positions for which you are qualified, in addition to identifying specific companies for which you would like to work.

Part of a job search is to determine in what city you want to work. If your job search is limited to your local area, you will be restricted to local employers. If you are willing to commute outside of your area, determine how far you are willing to commute (both directions) on a daily basis. If you wish to move out of the area, identify what locations are most appealing. Should you desire to move to a new location, do not forget to consider the cost of living in your desired location. The **cost of living** is the average cost of basic necessities such as housing, food, and clothing. For example, it is much more expensive to live in Manhattan, New York, than it is to live in Cheyenne, Wyoming. While a job in Manhattan may pay a lot more than a job in Cheyenne, living expenses typically justify the higher salary.

Exercise 2 Identify Target Employers

Identify your target work location and three companies/employers in your target location that may be of interest to you.

1.

2.

3.

Preparation

With the popularity of social networking sites, your personal life has a greater chance of being exposed in the job search process. Ensure you have a favorable **electronic image.** An electronic image is the image formed when someone is communicating with you and/or researching you through electronic means. This involves conducting an Internet search on you through personal pages and search engines. Since the majority of information on the Internet is public information, an increasing number of employers are conducting web searches on potential employees to gain a better perspective of the applicant's values and lifestyle. With today's overabundance of electronic social networking and information sites, personal blogs, and other file-sharing services, ensure that defamatory photos, writings, or other material will not be a barrier in your job search. When conducting an Internet search on yourself, remove any information that portrays you in a negative light. If you are actively involved in social networking sites, carefully evaluate any personal information that is contained on the sites of your friends. If negative information is contained on sites of your friends, explain your job search plans and politely ask them to remove the potentially harmful information.

An additional step toward ensuring a clean electronic image is to maintain a professional e-mail address. Sending a potential employer an e-mail from the address "prty2nite" is not the image you want to project. If necessary, establish a new e-mail address that utilizes some form of your name or initials to maintain a clean and professional electronic image. Two final considerations in maintaining a professional electronic image are the maintenance of a professional voice mail message and the avoidance of text slang in all written communication. Your job search strategy will involve extensive communication with employers and other individuals who will assist you with your job search. Interaction with these parties needs to be professional.

Talk It Out

What type of photos, writings, or materials do you think are inappropriate for a potential employer to see?

Job Search Portfolio

A **job search portfolio** is a collection of paperwork used for job searches. Some items from your job search portfolio will become a part of your interview portfolio. You will use the items you collect for your job search portfolio to keep you organized and prepared while searching for a job.

It is best to have a three-ring binder with tabs to keep all paperwork organized and protected. Do not punch holes in original documents. Place original documents in plastic notebook protectors. When you begin collecting items for your portfolio, keep the original and at least two copies of each item available at all times. These copies will be transferred to your interview portfolio when needed.

Because many of today's job searches occur over the Internet, it is also recommended you create an electronic job search portfolio. An **electronic job search portfolio** is a computerized folder that contains electronic copies of all job search documents. For your electronic job search file, scan copies of all documents you will be keeping in your hard-copy portfolio. When you share documents with potential employers and others over the Internet, these electronic documents will be sent as attachments.

A useful networking and introduction tool is a personal business card. A personal business card is a small card that contains contact information including your name, mailing and e-mail addresses, and phone number. It is a good practice to share your personal business card with anyone you meet, especially in networking, informational interview, and mentoring encounters. Doing so makes it easier for your new acquaintance to remember you and contact you in the future. Personal business cards are inexpensive and valuable networking tools and need not be professionally printed. Templates are available on the web and can easily be printed on cardstock paper, or you can purchase special business card packages online or at an office supply store. When designing a personal business card, ensure it contains all relevant contact information and reflects a professional image. Use an easy-to-read font style. Do not include fancy graphics, pictures, or too many words. Simple is better.

The following is a list of items to keep in your job search portfolio.

Item	Description
Network list	A list of professional relationships used for job contacts
Personal business cards	Cards with personal contact information used to share for job leads
Résumé	A formal profile that is presented to potential employers
Cover letter	Introduces a résumé
Reference list	A list of individuals who will provide a professional reference
Letters of recommendation	A written professional reference to verify work experience and character
Transcripts	Documents that verify education. Have both official (sealed) and copies available. Sealed transcripts may be required
Current state licenses	Documents that verify the ability to practice certain professions
Awards, certificates, work samples	Documents that demonstrate proficiency in specific skills
Completed generic application	Generic job application that makes information readily available
Copy of ID and/or driver's license	A valid ID and proof of ability to drive (if driving is a job requirement)
Copy of recent DMV record (if relevant to your career)	Used to ensure a safe driving record
Personal commercial	Statement that assists with interview
Small calendar, note pad, pen	To track important dates and make notes
Performance appraisals from previous jobs	Proof of positive work performance

Many careers that involve driving require a copy of your driving history. This information is secured by contacting your local Department of Motor Vehicles (DMV). If you have a poor driving record, check with your local DMV to identify how long this history stays on your record. Those with a blemished driving history may have a tougher time securing a job in a field that involves driving. When sharing your DMV record, as with all other portfolio items, provide only a copy (unless otherwise required) and maintain the original in your job search portfolio.

Employment Applications

Keep a completed generic employment application in your job search portfolio so you have required information readily available. If you have a smart phone, store this information on your device for quick and easy retrieval. When completing the application in its entirety, do not list your Social Security number or birth date. This information is not given to a prospective employer until you are a finalist for a job to protect against the potential of age discrimination and/or identity theft. Let the employer know you will supply this information upon hire.

An employment application is a legal document. When completing the application, read the fine print prior to signing the document. Commonly, at the end of the application, there will be a statement that grants the potential employer permission to conduct reference and various background checks, including a credit check if the information is relevant to the job for which you are applying. Fully understand why this background information is necessary and how it will be used in the hiring process. If you do not fully understand the statements on the application, clarify these statements prior to signing the application.

It is common for employers to request that the applicant complete an employment application and submit this document along with the résumé package. If you submitted only a cover letter and résumé, you may be asked to complete an application after you have been interviewed. Some employment applications can now be completed through a kiosk located at a worksite. Applications may also be downloaded, completed, and submitted directly from a target company's website. A keyboarded employment application is best. If keyboarding the application is not possible, complete the application by printing neatly in black ink. In some instances, after you have completed an online application, you may be asked to take a pre-employment test as part of the application process.

Personal References and Recommendations

Create a list of professional references that a potential employer can contact to verify your work experience and personal character. References are not to be included on your résumé. References are listed on a separate page. Do not send your reference list with your résumé unless it is requested by the employer. However, have a copy available to share if the employer requests references during the interview. Prior to including individuals on your reference list, ask each person if he or she is willing to serve as a reference. Be sure each person on this list will provide a positive reference. Have at least three names to submit as references. Include each reference's name, contact phone number, business mailing address, relationship, and e-mail address. References can be past or present employers and supervisors, coworkers, instructors, or someone with whom you have volunteered. Do not use relatives, friends, or religious leaders unless you have worked or volunteered with or for them.

In addition to reputable references, it is wise to have at least three **letters of recommendation.** A letter of recommendation is a written testimony from another person that states that you are credible. Letters of recommendation need to reflect current job skills, accomplishments, and positive human relations skills and should be no older than one year. Letters of recommendation can be from past or present employers, coworkers, instructors, or someone you worked for as a volunteer. It is common and acceptable to have someone write a formal letter of recommendation and serve as a personal reference.

In addition to routinely updating your résumé, keep your references list updated. Provide references relevant to your career. Occasionally check with your references and verify if they are still willing to serve as references. Keep these individuals current on your job search status and career goals.

Exercise 3 List Your References

List three people you can use as references. Then list three people you can ask to write you a letter of recommendation. Include their relationship to you.

Reference	Relationship
1.	
2.	
3.	

Letter of Recommendation	Relationship
1.	
2.	
3.	

Sources of Job Leads

There are many sources for job leads. Do not wait for potential employers to find you. Actively search association and employer sites of targeted industries. The most obvious job lead is directly from a targeted company. It is also acceptable to personally visit the target company's human resource department for current job announcements. If you do not have a targeted company but have a location where you would like to work, conduct an Internet search using the target city and target position as key search words. Search for associations in your targeted industry. They may offer online job banks. Many employers now post job announcements on social networking and corporate websites. Check online message boards and popular job search sites. Also, conduct key-word searches on community message boards. Keep track of the sites you are utilizing for your job search and monitor activity. Many larger cities and counties offer one-stop centers for job seekers. These government-funded agencies provide job-seeker assistance and serve as a link between job seekers and local employers. Other job sources include job fairs, newspaper advertisements, industry journals, and current employees who work in your targeted industry and/or company. Most individuals rely on posted job positions. However, many jobs are unsolicited (not advertised to the general public). The way to become aware of these unsolicited jobs is to use your professional network. The larger your professional network, the more you will become aware of unannounced job leads. A discussion on how to create and utilize a professional network is presented later in this chapter. Once you have established a network, inform network members of your desire for a job and ask for potential job leads.

Treat all face-to-face job search situations, including distributing your résumé, meeting a potential network contact, or visiting a company to identify open positions, as if you are going to an interview. Dress professionally, go alone, have extra copies of your résumé, display confidence, and bring your interview portfolio. In networking situations where there are many job seekers, such as a job fair, be polite and professional in your interactions with everyone. Do not interrupt or be rude to other job seekers. Take the lead in introducing yourself to company representatives. Sell your skills and confidently ask the company representative if he or she has an open position requiring your skills. Your goal in such a situation is to favorably stand out from the crowd, share your résumé, and arrange an interview. There are situations where applicants are invited to "on the spot" interviews. Your professional appearance and interview portfolio will show that you are prepared. Dressing casually and/or having a child or friend in tow will communicate unprofessionalism to a potential employer.

If you are unable to find a job lead, send an unsolicited cover letter and résumé to your target company either electronically or through traditional mail. When sending an unsolicited résumé, send two copies: one to the human resource manager, and the other to the manager of your target job. Prior to sending your résumé, call the company to secure the names of both individuals. Ensure you have identified the correct spelling and gender for the individuals to whom you will be sending your résumé. Sending two résumés to the same company increases the opportunity of securing an interview. The targeted department manager will most likely read and file your résumé for future reference. The human resource manager will also review your résumé and may identify other jobs for which you are qualified.

Networking

During the time you will be looking for a job or advanced position, establishing a professional network is important—as is maintaining this network throughout your career. **Networking** is the act of creating professional relationships. Think of networking as a connection device. The purpose of creating a professional network is to have a resource of individuals whom you can call upon for professional assistance and/or advice. While the intent of this discussion is to utilize a professional network for job search purposes, a professional network is also a useful tool for collaborating and assisting others.

Professional networking is necessary throughout a job search. There are two primary forms of networking. The first form is the traditional method, which involves face-to-face interaction. The second method utilizes social media. Traditional networking involves interacting with and meeting as many people as possible who work or know someone who works in your targeted industry. There are many formal networking opportunities for job seekers, including attending association meetings, service clubs, and conferences or trade shows. Additionally, many college career centers provide networking events for students to interact with local employers. Job fairs, volunteer fairs, and trade shows are excellent venues for professional networking. The key to successful networking is to begin creating a network before you need one. This provides you time to develop your networking skills, increase your confidence, and identify which venues work best. Many college recruiters enjoy meeting students a year prior to graduation. Students who are networking early in their job search convey organization, planning, and strategic skills, which are skills highly desired by employers.

Developing a professional network is easy. You inform one person that you are looking for a job. That person informs others, then those people inform

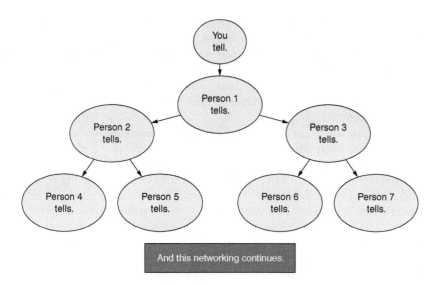

Figure 1

Networking

others, and soon you have many people who know that you are searching for a job. View Figure 1 to see how a network grows.

Almost every person you know may be a part of your network, including coworkers, supervisors, instructors, family, and friends.

Cory has been working as an account clerk for a year. During this year, Cory has acquired new accounting skills, has learned new software packages, and has graduated with an accounting degree. Cory begins by telling supervisors and coworkers what skills and education have been acquired. In addition, Cory mentions the new skills and software packages learned over the last year and shares future goals. Cory then tells family members and friends the same information. This is the beginning of Cory's professional network. Cory creates a network list and begins tracking and updating these people. Cory will continue to update the people on the network list about new skills acquired and job search progress.

When engaging in traditional networking, remember that the success of one's networking attempts begin with a positive attitude. Review what you have learned in previous chapters of this text regarding professional behavior. First and foremost, believe in yourself and your abilities. Be confident and willing to approach and initiate an introduction with strangers. People are drawn to positive people. When actively networking, dress professionally, because first impressions matter. Have both your personal business card and a brief statement of your key skills to informally share with anyone you meet. When you share a business card, ask for one in return. Obtaining the card provides you the opportunity to follow up. Also use the information from your new contact's business card to update your network list. Practice the art of introducing yourself in a positive and professional manner, beginning with a professional handshake. Listen carefully to the name of the individual you are meeting. After the handshake, exchange business cards. Prior to telling your new contact about you and your job search, ask about him or her. Get the individual to talk about where he or she works, what he or she does, and what he or she enjoys about the job. Use this time to build rapport. At the appropriate time, tell the individual about you and your job search. As your conversation continues, watch for body-language cues. If the person is engaged, he or she will make direct eye contact and turn his or her body toward you. If the person does not want to visit too long, he or she will look away and/or turn his or her body away from you. Utilize these cues to either continue the visit or politely thank him or her for the visit and end the conversation.

While it is common to have food and beverages available at formal networking events, it is best to refrain from eating and drinking until you have met your desired network contacts. Practice proper etiquette by not overindulging in food items. You are in attendance to meet people, not to eat. It is always best to refrain from drinking alcohol.

There are also other methods to expand your network, such as volunteering for community organizations. Volunteering provides a chance to meet people in different organizations and learn about new positions throughout the community. Volunteering is an excellent venue to develop leadership and team-building skills, network, and, most importantly, give back to your community. Join clubs and professional organizations. Attend workshops, conferences, and seminars to meet people from corporations that are in your targeted career field.

Current technologies now provide ample social media outlets to not only post your résumé to targeted industries, but also to create an electronic network. Some popular online professional networking venues are LinkedIn and Facebook. Both of these venues have special support services for job seekers, but there are many industry-specific networking venues online. When utilizing a social networking site for your job search, ensure that your career information is current and consistent with your résumé. However, be cautious when sharing personal information over these venues.

Within twenty-four hours of a networking experience, follow up with a brief message telling the individual that it was a pleasure meeting him or her. Attach your résumé to your message, and tell your new contact to feel free to pass your résumé along to others. If you are interested in conducting an informational interview with your new contact, do not attach your résumé. The purpose of your message will be to not only thank the individual for his or her time, but also to ask for and arrange an informational interview. An **informational interview** is when a job seeker meets with a business professional to learn about a specific career, company, or industry. You are not asking for a job during an informational interview. You are only expanding your professional network. During an informational interview, ask the business professional questions about targeted careers, hiring, and the culture of the company. By meeting and talking with business professionals, you have increased your professional network. When you network, do not be afraid to ask those with whom you network for additional contacts who may be able to assist you. Networking involves giving and taking. If you read an industry-related article, attend a conference, or are working on a project that may interest someone in your network, share the information and demonstrate how you can be of value to them.

Talk It Out

What is appropriate and inappropriate information to share when creating an online network?

Exercise 4   Identify Your Current Network

Where have you met people who you can include in your professional network?

1. _____

2. _____

3. _____

Create and maintain a network list. A **network list** is an easily accessible list of all network contacts' names, industries, addresses, and phone numbers so you can contact each person for quick reference. Provide each contact who is actively assisting with your job search a copy of your most current résumé. Keep all contacts on your network list updated throughout your job search. When keeping in contact with members of your network, be sensitive to their time. Do not annoy them or be inconsiderate in your interactions. Ensure that your network contact list is up-to-date. Find and consistently utilize a database system that is convenient for you. Most individuals use an electronic database, while some still prefer a traditional address book. Whatever you use, keep it current. If you find a job, immediately remove job search postings and inform members of your network who were actively assisting you with your search for a job.

Networking for both business and job search purposes is work, but the effort reaps tremendous benefits if done appropriately. Every few months, review your professional network list. If there is someone with whom you have not recently connected, contact him or her to say hello and keep him or her updated on your career and growth plans.

Protecting Your Privacy

The job search process involves sharing personal information. Be cautious and share only personal information with reputable sources or you may become a target for identity theft. If you are applying for a job and have never heard of the employer, conduct research to verify that the employer is legitimate. As stated earlier, do not share your birth date or Social Security number with any employer until after you are a finalist for the job.

Cory's friend Terry was looking for a job. Terry found a job on an online classified job site that sounded legitimate. The employer asked that Terry submit a résumé online. Within a few days after sharing his résumé, Terry received an e-mail telling him that he was a finalist for the job. The only step left in the process was for Terry to forward a copy of his credit report. Although Terry was desperate for a job, he thought this was a little strange, so he asked Cory what Cory thought of the situation. Cory conducted an Internet search for Terry and could not find any evidence that the company Terry was applying to even existed. Cory asked Terry if he completed an application that gave the potential employer permission to view Terry's credit information, and Terry said no. Cory and Terry agreed that sharing personal information with an unknown company was not a good idea.

Keeping the Right Attitude

The importance of maintaining a positive attitude throughout your career cannot be stressed enough. This holds true during your job search. The job search process is a lot of work and can sometimes be frustrating. Do not get discouraged if you do not get an interview or job offer on your first try. In tight job markets, it may take many interviews before receiving a job offer.

To maintain a healthy attitude during this time of transition, follow these tips when looking for a job:

1. *Stay positive:* Start each day with a positive affirmation. Speaking aloud, tell yourself that you are a talented and great person who deserves a good job (and believe what you say). Your attitude is reflected in your actions. If you allow negative elements to influence your job search, you will be at a disadvantage.

2. *Stay active:* Create a daily and weekly "to do" list. Every day, check the websites of your targeted industries, associations, and companies in addition to checking relevant job sites. Schedule time for industry and company research, as well as time for networking. A job search is a job in itself. You do not want to be an unproductive employee in the workplace, so begin creating good work habits now by making the most of your time in a job search.

3. *Keep learning:* Use job search down time to learn or develop a skill. As with your routine industry and company research and daily review of targeted job postings, schedule learning time. Identify a skill that will assist you when you are offered a job. Finances do not have to be a barrier to learning new skills. There are many free tutorials available on the Internet. Topics to consider include computer skills, writing skills, or any skill specific to your chosen industry.

4. *Stay connected:* Although it is natural to not want to socialize with others when discouraged, the job search period is the time when you most need to be in the presence of others. In addition to keeping your current network updated on your job search, identify further reasons to communicate with your network. Consistently work on expanding your network by attending association meetings and events, volunteering, and scheduling informational interviews. Plan at least one meeting and/or activity each day. As opposed to sitting around the house waiting for the phone to ring, dressing professionally and networking every day will contribute to your maintaining a positive outlook.

5. *Stay focused:* During this time of transition, manage your professional job search, your personal health, and your environment. Manage your professional job search by maintaining an up-to-date calendar with scheduled follow-up activities relating to your job search. Because a job search is a stressful experience, practice healthy stress management techniques, including a proper diet, regular exercise, and positive self-talk. Invest a portion of your time in something of interest other than your job search. Consider volunteering for an organization of special interest to you. Doing so will provide a mental break, provide possible new network contacts, and provide you the satisfaction of helping others. Managing your personal environment involves making wise choices regarding personal finances. Be cautious and conservative with your money. Make thoughtful purchases and avoid emotional spending. Finally, surround yourself with individuals who are positive and supportive of you and your efforts.

If you are currently working and you begin looking for a new job, keep your job search confidential. If you are listing your supervisor as a reference, let him or her know you are looking for a new job and briefly explain why. Do not quit your current job before accepting a new job. Also, do not bad-mouth your company or anyone who works for your current or former employer(s).

Workplace Dos and Don'ts

Do keep your original job search documents in a portfolio	*Don't* give employers your original documents and expect them to be returned to you
Do keep a network list and keep the people on your list updated	*Don't* be annoying or inconsiderate of your network contacts' time
Do realize that a targeted job search takes time	*Don't* get discouraged if you do not get an interview or job offer on your first try
Do explore various sources of job leads, including your personal network, the Internet, and industry journals	*Don't* limit your job leads to one source

Concept Review and Application

Summary of Key Concepts

- The career objective or personal profile is a brief statement that sells your key skills and relates to your self-discovery
- A targeted job search leads you through the process of identifying open positions for which you are qualified, in addition to identifying companies for which you would like to work
- Ensure you have a professional electronic image while job searching
- Professional networking is the act of creating professional relationships
- In addition to people you already know, develop additional network contacts through various sources of job leads
- Creating and maintaining a job search portfolio will keep you organized and prepared during the job search process
- Create a list of professional references for employers

Key Terms

career objective
electronic job
  search portfolio
networking
self-discovery

cost of living
informational interviews
letters of
  recommendation
targeted job search

electronic image
job search portfolio
network list
personal profile

If You Were the Boss

1. What information would you supply to a job seeker during an informational interview with you?
2. If you discovered that one of your top interview candidates had an unprofessional website, what would you do?

Video Case Study: Job Fair

Pearson Education

This video addresses inappropriate and appropriate behavior when participating in a job fair. To view these videos, visit the Student Resources: Professionalism section in www.mystudentsuccesslab.com. Then answer the following questions:

1. What inappropriate behaviors did Kevin exhibit at the job fair? Be specific in your answer.
2. What inappropriate behaviors did Sean exhibit at the job fair? Be specific in your answer.
3. What appropriate behaviors did Rachel exhibit at the job fair? Be specific in your answer.
4. Did Rachel close her interview appropriately? Why or why not?

Video Case Study: Job Search Strategies

This video presents expert advice on how to conduct a professional job search. To view these videos, visit the Student Resources: Professionalism section in www.mystudentsuccesslab.com. Then answer the following questions:

1. What are important considerations and activities that should take place during the research phase of a job search?
2. What is a network, and how do you create it?
3. What specific advice does the expert provide regarding cold-call applications?

Web Links

http://www.rileyguide.com/network.html#netprep
http://jobsearch.about.com/od/networking
http://www.truecareers.com
http://www.weddles.com/associations/index.cfm
http://money.cnn.com/magazines/fortune/rankings/
http://www.glassdoor.com/index.htm

Activities

Activity 1

Create a reference list with at least three names; include the following information.

Reference 1
Name
Job title
Place of employment
Address
Telephone number
E-mail address
Relationship (why is he or she a reference?)
Reference 2
Name
Job title
Place of employment
Address
Telephone number
E-mail address
Relationship (why is he or she a reference?)
Reference 3
Name
Job title
Place of employment
Address
Telephone number
E-mail address
Relationship (why is he or she a reference?)

Activity 2

Using the following network table to create a networking list.

NETWORK TABLE				
Network List				
Name	Address	Phone No.	E-Mail Address	Last Date of Contact

Activity 3

Using an Internet job site or other job sources, identify three specific job titles that match your career goals and current qualifications.

Job Titles
1.
2.
3.

Activity 4

Design a personal business card.

Activity 5

Secure a job application online or from a local employer. With the exception of your signature, complete the application. Include this document in your job search portfolio.

1. The act of creating professional relationships is referred to as _____.

2. The following people could be included in a professional network:

   _____,

   _____,

   _____,

   _____, and

   _____.

3. One of the most obvious job sources is utilizing your _____.

4. Keep your phone message _____.

5. The process of identifying your key interests and skills built upon career goals is known as

   _____.

6. The _____ or _____ is an introductory written statement

   at the beginning of a résumé.

7. A _____ is an image formed when someone is researching you through a

   computer search.

8. An employment application is a _____.

Suggested Readings

Beagrie, S. "How to Jump-Start Your Job Search," Personnel Today (January 8, 2008): 5.

"Nearly Half of Empoyers Use Social Media to Research Candidates," *HR Focus* 86 (December 2009): 8.

Benezine, K. "Applying for Jobs," *Caterer & Hotelkeeper* (2009 Careers Guide): 4–5.

"Feds Turning Up Heat on HR Background Checks," HR Specialists: *Employment Law* 40 (May 2010): 1–2.

Interview Techniques

George Doyle / Thinkstock

All the world's a stage.

William Shakespeare (1564–1616)

MyStudentSuccessLab Visit www.mystudentsuccesslab.com for added practice, activities, assessment, and videos.

From Chapter 15 of *Professionalism: Skills for Workplace Success*, Third Edition. Lydia E. Anderson, Sandra B. Bolt.

Objectives

- Demonstrate strategies to implement when invited to interview
- Conduct company and job-specific research for interview preparation
- Prepare a *personal commercial* to sell skills and tie them to a target job
- Identify pre-interview preparation activities including creating an *interview portfolio* and practice interview questions
- Demonstrate how to behave during technology-based interviews
- Explain key areas of employee rights and how to respond to discriminatory questions
- Describe specific statements and behaviors to exhibit at the close of an interview and job offer
- Discuss salary negotiation strategies

How-Do-You-Rate

	Have you mastered interview techniques?	True	False
1.	Arriving more than ten minutes early to the office where your interview is to take place is considered unprofessional.	❏	❏
2.	It is best to have a draft of a post-interview thank-you note written prior to an interview.	❏	❏
3.	The same amount of pre-interview preparation should be made for an Internet and/or telephone interview as is made for a traditional face-to-face interview.	❏	❏
4.	Employers expect a job candidate to ask valid questions during interviews.	❏	❏
5.	When offered a job, it is acceptable to negotiate a salary for entry-level positions.	❏	❏

If you answered "true" to the majority of these questions, congratulations. You are already aware of successful interview techniques and are ready to successfully interview.

The Interview

You've conducted a targeted job search, and created and distributed your résumé, and now it is time to interview. A successful interview involves more than dressing sharp. It includes advance preparation; confidence; and a strategy to be used before, during, and after this important meeting. During an interview, an employer is looking to hire the best person to represent his or her company. Your goal is to communicate visually and verbally that you are the right person for the job. A job search takes work, takes time, and can sometimes be frustrating. Do not get discouraged if you do not get an interview or job offer on your first try. The purpose of this chapter is to provide you the skills and confidence to secure a good job in a reasonable time period.

The Invitation to Interview

There is a strategy to successful interviews, and it starts as soon as you receive an invitation to interview. Most interview invitations are extended by phone or electronic mail. Therefore, regularly check and respond to both phone and electronic messages. This is a good reminder to maintain a professional voice-mail message and e-mail address. When you are invited to interview, attempt to identify with whom you will be interviewing. You may be meeting with one person or a group of individuals. Your first interview may be a pre-screening interview where a human resource representative or some other representative from the company briefly meets with you to ensure you are qualified and the right fit for the job.

Ask how much time the company has scheduled for the interview. If possible, identify how many applicants are being called for interviews. Although this is a lot of information to secure, if you are friendly, respectful, and professional, most companies will share this information. Attempt to arrange your interview at a time that puts you at an advantage over the other candidates. The first and last interviews are the most memorable, so try to be the first or last interview. If you are given a choice of times to interview, schedule your interview in the morning. People are much more alert at that time, and you will have a greater advantage of making a favorable and memorable impression. If this is not possible, try to be the last person interviewed prior to the lunch break or the first person interviewed immediately after the lunch break. Be aware that sometimes you will have no say in when your interview is scheduled. Do not make demands when scheduling your interview. Politely ask the interview scheduler if it is possible for him or her to tell you who will be conducting the interview. Finally, note the name of the individual who is assisting you in arranging the interview. This will allow you to contact him or her should you need information and also allow you to personally thank him or her if you meet on the day of the interview. The goal is to secure as much information as possible prior to the interview so you are prepared.

Company-Specific Research

Prior to your interview, conduct research on the company and the specific position for which you are applying. Many candidates ignore this step, thinking it is unnecessary or takes too much time. Planning better prepares you for your interview, increases your confidence, and provides you a greater advantage over other candidates. Learn as much as you can about the company's leadership team, strategy, and any current event that may have affected the company. Review the company web and social network sites if available, or conduct a general Internet search to read blogs and other posts related to the company. Note products the company produces, identify the company's key competitors, and note any recent community activities or recognized accomplishments the company has been involved with.

In addition to the Internet, other sources for securing company information include company-produced brochures/literature, industry journals, and interviews with current employees and business leaders. Job-specific information is easily gathered by conducting a quick search on the O*Net database using the position title as your key word. As mentioned in the résumé chapter, this database of occupational information provides key information by job title.

The pre-interview research will assist you during your job interview. Identify as much as you can about the company, its administrators, and the department of your target job. Not only will you have an advantage in the interview, but you will know if this company is the right fit for you and your career goals. Use the company-specific research information to tailor your résumé, cover letter, and interview responses. This provides you an advantage over others who do not research the company.

In your interview, mention specific information about the company. This shows you have conducted research. For example, a popular interview question is, "Why do you want to work for this company?" If you have conducted research, be specific in your answer and respond with information that reflects your research. For example, say, "Your company has been green-conscious in the last two years, which is an area I, too, believe is important," instead of saying, "I have heard it is a great company."

Cory's friend Tomasz was excited about an interview he would be having in a week. When Tomasz was sharing his excitement with Cory, Cory asked him if he had conducted research on the company. Tomasz said he really didn't need to conduct research because the company was pretty well known. Cory explained that it was important to conduct research beyond general knowledge to make sure Tomasz stood out from the other candidates. Cory and Tomasz conducted an extensive Internet search on the target company, and Tomasz discovered useful information that Tomasz was able to use throughout his interview. After a successful interview, Tomasz thanked Cory and told Cory that the research prior to his interview gave him a lot of confidence that ultimately helped him secure the job.

The Personal Commercial

Prepare a **personal commercial** that sells your skills and ties these skills to the specific job for which you are interviewing. A personal commercial is a brief career biography that conveys your career choice, knowledge, skills, strengths, abilities, and experiences that make you uniquely qualified for the position for which you are applying. Include your interest in the targeted position, and use this personal commercial at the beginning or end of an interview. The purpose of the commercial is to sell your skills in a brief statement. Your goal is to sell yourself and match your skills to fit the company needs by adapting them to the requirements for each target job. Your personal commercial is essentially your "sales pitch" that communicates your key and unique knowledge, skills, and abilities that make you the right choice for your target job.

Exercise 1   Communicating Key Information

If you were alone in an elevator with the hiring manager of your target job, what key pieces of information would you communicate about yourself as you rode from the fifth floor to the first floor?

Do not include marital status, hobbies, or other personal information in your personal commercial. When you write your personal commercial make it reflect your personality. Include your interest in your chosen career, activities related to the career, the skills you have acquired, and why you have enjoyed learning these skills. Your personal commercial should take no more than two minute to deliver. The following is an example of a personal commercial.

Personal Commercial Example

Since I can remember, I have been interested in math, numbers, and counting money. In junior high, I started myself on a budget and kept track of saving and spending. By high school I knew I wanted to become an accountant.

After finishing my classes at our local community college, I started working as an account clerk for a hospital. In addition to my regular duties, I was able to attend conferences and workshops where I expanded my knowledge and skills in different areas of accounting.

I am a recent college graduate from State University, where I received a bachelor's of science in accounting. With the additional education, I utilized these new skills and knowledge to work with general ledgers, accounts payable, and accounts receivable. I plan to apply my abilities and improve constantly.

With my experience as an Account Clerk, I have developed soft skills including how to deal with customers and coworkers in good and bad situations. In addition to the skills I have obtained working with MAS 90, I am proficient in MS Word and Excel. I have basic skills with Access, Outlook, and PowerPoint.

My goal is to become a CPA. Your company will benefit from my work ethic, which is to give 100 percent of my ability to all clients and provide them the confidence they need for someone handling their money. My values include integrity and innovation. I am organized, dedicated, responsible, punctual, and willing to learn. I believe I am the best candidate for this position. Since your company is committed to clients and the community, I would like to be a part of your team.

Exercise 2   Starting a Personal Commercial

Identify key points to include in your personal commercial.

_____

_____

_____

_____

_____

_____

Use your personal commercial during your interview when asked, "Tell me about yourself." If you are not given this instruction during the interview, include your personal commercial at the end of the interview. Practice delivering your commercial in front of a mirror.

The Interview Portfolio

An **interview portfolio** is a small folder containing relevant documents that are taken to an interview. Use a professional looking business portfolio or paper folder with pockets for your interview portfolio. Include copies of items pertinent to the position for which you are applying. Original documents (unless required) should not be given to the employer, only photocopies. Have the following items in your interview portfolio: copies of résumé, cover letter, reference list, generic application, and personal commercial. Also, include a calendar, note paper, a pen, and personal business cards. Print copies of your résumé, cover letter, and references on résumé paper. Copies of other items such as skill or education certificates and recent performance evaluations may be included if the information is relevant to the job. Keep your interview portfolio on your lap during the interview. Place your personal commercial on the top of your portfolio for easy access. Do not read the commercial. You may glance at it if you become nervous and forget what to say.

Practice Interview Questions

Another activity when preparing for an interview is to practice interview questions. Table 1 identifies common interview questions, the purpose of each question, and an appropriate way to answer each question. Review this list and begin creating appropriate responses to each question. Whenever you are answering interview questions, be honest and provide examples of specific skills and experiences that support your answers and meet the key requirements of the target job. The more real-life examples you provide, the more you demonstrate your experience and skill level to the employer. Anyone can say, "I can handle stress on a busy day"; however, by providing a specific example of how you handled stress on a busy day, you have demonstrated how you realistically handle stress.

Practice answering interview questions in front of a mirror, and, if possible, create a practice interview video of yourself answering common interview questions. Critically analyze your responses to see if you are appropriately answering the questions, selling your key skills, and projecting a professional image. Also check for nervous gestures. Doing this will better prepare you for an interview and help increase your self-confidence.

> **Talk It Out**
>
> Identify the most difficult questions to answer, and formulate appropriate responses that sell your skills.

Pre-Interview Practice

Prior to the day of your interview, visit the interview location, pre-plan your interview wardrobe, ensure your interview portfolio is up-to-date, and prepare post-interview thank-you notes.

Conduct a "practice day" prior to the day of your interview. If possible, drive or find transportation to the interview location. Ideally, do this on the same hour as your scheduled interview to identify potential transportation problems including traffic and parking. Once at the site, walk to the location where the interview will be held. This will enable you to become comfortable and familiar with your surroundings and let you know how much time you will

Table 1	Common Interview Questions	
Question	**Answer**	**Do Not**
Tell me about yourself.	Use your personal commercial modified to the job description.	Do not divulge where you were born, hobbies, or other personal information.
What are your strengths?	Include how your strengths meet the job requirements and how they will be an asset to the company.	Do not include strengths that are not related to the job. Do not include personal information (e.g., "I'm a good mother").
Tell me about a time you failed.	Use an example that is not too damaging. Turn it into a positive by including the lesson learned from your mistake.	Do not exclude the lesson learned from the failure. Do not place blame for why the failure occurred.
Tell me about a time you were successful.	Use an example that relates to the job for which you are applying.	Do not take full credit if the success was a team effort.
How do you handle conflict?	Use an example that is not too damaging. Include how the conflict was positively resolved.	Do not provide specifics on how the conflict occurred, and do not use a negative example or place blame on others.
Would you rather work individually or in a team? Why?	State that you prefer one or the other and why, but relate your answer to the job requirements.	Do not state that you will not work one way or the other.
Why do you want this job?	Convey career goals and how the job supports your current skills. Include company information learned through research.	Do not state money or benefits in your response.
How do you deal with stress?	Share positive stress reducers.	Do not state that stress does not affect you. Do not use negative examples.
What is your greatest weakness?	Use a weakness that will not damage your chance of getting the job. Explain how you are minimizing your weakness or are turning it into a strength (e.g., "I'm a perfectionist, but I don't allow it to interfere with getting my job done on time").	Do not state, "I don't have any."
Where do you want to be in five years?	Share your career goals.	Do not say you want the interviewer's job.
Tell me about a time you displayed leadership.	Use a specific example, and try to relate the example to the needed job skills.	Do not appear arrogant.

need to arrive at the interview on time. Do not go into the specific office, just the general area. Make note of the nearest public restroom so you can use it the day of the interview to freshen up prior to your meeting.

Ensure that your interview attire is clean and professional prior to the day of the interview. Dress at a level above the position for which you are interviewing. For example, if you are interviewing for an entry-level position, dress like you are interviewing for a supervisor position. Check that your clothes are spotless and fit appropriately and your shoes are clean. Women, if relevant, it is a good idea to have an extra pair of nylons available in case of snags or tears. Ensure that your hair and fingernails are professional and appropriate for an interview. If necessary, get a haircut prior to your interview. Use little or no perfume/aftershave and keep jewelry to a minimum. Cleanliness is important.

Prior to the interview, customize your interview portfolio for the target job. Place your portfolio in a place where you will not forget it when you leave your home.

Purchase a package of simple but professional thank-you notes. The evening before your interview, write a draft thank-you note on a blank piece of paper. Keep your thank-you note brief, only three to four sentences. In the note, thank the interviewer for his or her time. State that you enjoyed learning more about the position, are very interested in the job, and look forward to hearing from the interviewer soon. This draft note will be used as a foundation for notes you will be writing immediately after your interview. Place the draft note, the package of thank-you notes, and a black pen alongside your interview portfolio to take with you.

Exercise 3 Thank-You Note

Write a draft thank-you note.

The Day of the Interview

Be well rested and have food in your stomach prior to leaving your home for the interview. Look in the mirror to check your appearance and clothing. Your clothes should fit properly and project a professional image. If you smoke, refrain from smoking prior to the interview. The smell may be a distraction to the interviewer.

Plan to arrive at your destination fifteen minutes early. This provides time to deal with unforeseen traffic and/or parking issues. If there is a public restroom available, go to the restroom and freshen up. Check your hair, clothing, and makeup, if applicable. Turn off your phone, and if you are chewing gum, throw it away. Enter the specific meeting location five minutes prior to your scheduled interview. This is where your interview unofficially begins. First impressions matter, and any interaction with representatives of the organization must be professional.

Immediately upon entering the interview location, introduce yourself to the receptionist. Offer a smile and a handshake, and then clearly and slowly state your name. For example, "Hi, I'm Cory Kringle, and I am here for a 9:00 a.m. interview with Ms. Dancey for the accounting clerk position." If you recognize the receptionist as the same individual who arranged your interview appointment, make an additional statement thanking the individual for his or her assistance. For example, "Mrs. Wong, were you the one that I spoke with on the phone? Thank you for your help in arranging my interview." Be sincere in your conversation, and convey to the receptionist that you appreciate his or her efforts. The receptionist will most likely ask you to have a seat and wait to be called into the interview. Take a seat and relax. While you are waiting, use **positive self-talk.** Positive self-talk is a mental form of positive self-reinforcement. It helps remind you that you are qualified and deserve both the interview and the job. Mentally tell yourself that you are prepared, qualified, and ready for a successful interview. Review your personal commercial, your qualifications, and the key skills you want to convey in the interview.

Cory's friend Shelby had been asked to interview with one of her target companies. Shelby really wanted the job but was afraid she was not going to do well during her interview. Cory worked with Shelby the evening before the interview by role-playing interview questions and reviewing Shelby's company research. The next day, when Shelby arrived for the interview, she arrived early, thanked the receptionist, and took a seat. As Shelby waited to be called in to the interview, she began getting extremely nervous. Remembering Cory's tips, Shelby briefly closed her eyes and used positive self-talk to improve her attitude, increase her confidence, and calm her nerves. After doing this, she felt more confident when called into the office to begin the interview.

The Interview

During an interview, communicate confidence. Your primary message during the interview will be how your knowledge, skills, and abilities will be assets to the company. When you are called to interview, stand up and approach the individual who called your name. If it is not the receptionist who called you, extend a smile and a handshake, then clearly and slowly state your name. For example, "Hi, I'm Cory Kringle. It's nice to meet you." Listen carefully to the interviewer's name so you will remember it and use it during the interview. He or she will escort you to an office or conference room where the interview will take place. If you enter a room and there is someone in the room that you have not met, smile, extend a handshake, and introduce yourself. Once in the room, do not be seated until you are invited to do so. When seated, if possible, write down the names of the individuals you have just met. Inject the interviewer's name(s) during the interview. Although you may be offered something to drink, it is best to decline the offer so there is nothing to distract you from the interview. If you are sitting in a chair that swivels, put your feet flat on the floor to remind yourself not to swivel. If you forgot to turn off your phone and it rings during the interview, do not answer the phone. Immediately, apologize to the employer and turn it off.

The interview may be conducted different ways. It may involve only one person, it may involve several individuals, it may involve testing, or it may be a combination of interviewing and testing. Testing activities must be job-related, such as typing tests for office work, lifting for a warehouse position, or demonstrating other skills that are included in the job requirements and/or job duties. If the interview is taking place in an office, look around the room to get a sense of the person who is conducting the interview, assuming it is his or her office. This provides useful information for conversation, should it be necessary. Depending on the time available and the skills of the interviewer(s), you may first be asked general questions, such as, "Did you have trouble finding our office?" The interviewer is trying to get you to relax. During the interview, pay attention to body language—both yours and that of the individual conducting the interview. Sit up straight, sit back in your chair, and try to relax. Be calm but alert. Keep your hands folded on your lap or ready to take notes, depending on the situation. If you are seated near a desk or table, do not lean on the furniture. Make eye contact, but do not stare at the interviewer.

If you are given the opportunity to provide an opening statement, share your personal commercial. If you are not able to open with your personal commercial, include it in an appropriate response or use it at the end of the interview. When asked a question, listen carefully. Take a few seconds to think and digest what information the interviewer truly wants to know about your skill sets. Formulate an answer. Interview answers should relate back to the job qualifications and/or job duties. Your goal is to convey to the interviewer how your skills will assist the company in achieving success. Keep your answers brief but complete. Sell your skills and expertise by including a specific but short example. Whenever possible, inject information you learned about the company during your research.

Phone- and other Technology-Based Interviews

In some situations, your first interview may take place over the phone. Phone interviews may occur without prearrangement, while others are scheduled. During your job search, consistently answer your phone(s) in a professional manner and keep your interview portfolio in an accessible place. If a company calls and asks if it is a good time to speak with you and it is not, politely respond that it is not a good time and ask if you can reschedule the call. Try to be as accommodating as possible to the interviewer.

Those being interviewed by phone should follow these tips:

- *Be professional and be prepared.* Conduct the interview in a quiet room. Remove all distractions, including music, pets, television, and other individuals from your quiet area. Company research, personal examples, and the use of your personal commercial are just as important to inject into the phone conversation as during a face-to-face interview. Just as in a face-to-face interview, take notes and ask questions.

- *Be concise with your communication.* Those conducting the interview are not able to see you; therefore, they are forming an impression of you by what you say and how it is stated. Speak clearly and slowly, and do not interrupt. Smile while you speak, and speak with enthusiasm. Use proper grammar and beware of "ums" and other nervous verbal phrases. If you stand while conducting your phone interview, you will keep alert, focused, and more aware of your responses.
- *Be polite.* Exercise good manners. Do not eat or chew gum during your interview. It is not appropriate to use a speaker phone when being interviewed, nor is it polite to take another call, or tend to personal matters. Your attention should be completely focused on the interview. When the conversation is over, ask for the job, and thank the interviewer for his or her time.

Due to a tight economy, it is becoming increasingly common for interviews to take place through video chat venues such as Skype, WebEx, and Google Talk. An individual participating in a video chat interview needs a computer, a web cam, and a reliable Internet connection. When taking part in a video chat interview, the participant will receive a designated time and specific instructions on where and how to establish the connection. In addition to following the phone interview tips, the interviewer needs to prepare and treat the video chat interview as if it were a face-to-face interview. Therefore,

- *Plan ahead.* Research the venue you will be using to address any unforeseen issues. Identify where you will conduct the interview and what technology is required. If possible, arrange a pre-interview trial to ensure all equipment works properly and you know how to use it (including your volume and microphone).
- *Dress professionally.* You will be in plain view of the interviewer, so visual impressions matter.
- *Maintain a professional environment.* Conduct your interview in a quiet and appropriate location. A bedroom, public place, or outside location is not appropriate.
- *Speak to the camera.* Focus on the web cam as if it were the interviewer's face. Feel free to ask questions, take notes, and use hand gestures. While it may be more difficult to communicate, make every effort to not only project your personality, but, more importantly, sell your knowledge, skills, abilities, and unique qualifications. As with a traditional face-to-face interview, your job is to connect with the interviewer.

Interview Methods and Types of Interview Questions

There are several common types of interviews. These include one-on-one interviews, group interviews, and panel interviews. **One-on-one interviews** involve a one-on-one meeting between the applicant and a company representative. The company representative is typically either someone from the human resource department or the immediate supervisor of the department with the open position.

Group interviews involve several applicants interviewing with each other while being observed by company representatives. The purpose of a group interview is to gauge how an individual behaves in a competitive and stressful environment. In a group interview situation, practice positive human relation and communication skills toward other applicants. Listening and communicating that you are the best candidate is critical to a successful group interview. If another applicant is first asked a question and you are immediately asked the same question, do not repeat what the other applicant said. If you agree with the first applicant's response, state, "I agree with Ms. Bell's response and would like to add that it's also important to...," and then elaborate or expand on the first applicant's response. If you do not agree with the first applicant's response, state, "I believe...," and then confidently provide your response. Do not demean other applicants. Be professional, do not interrupt, and behave like a leader. Be assertive, not aggressive.

Panel interviews involve the applicant meeting with several company employees at the same time. During a panel interview, make initial eye contact with the person asking the question. While answering the question, make eye contact with the other members of the interview panel. Whenever possible, call individuals by name.

The three general types of interview questions are structured, unstructured, and behavioral. **Structured interview questions** address job-related issues where each applicant is asked the same question(s). An example of a structured question is, "How long have you worked in the retail industry?" The purpose of a structured interview question is to secure information related to a specific job. An **unstructured interview question** is a probing, open-ended question. The purpose of an unstructured interview question is to identify if the candidate can appropriately sell his or her skills. An example of an unstructured interview question is, "Tell me about yourself." When you are asked to talk about yourself, state your personal commercial. This is where you begin using the interview portfolio. Whenever possible, pull job samples from your interview portfolio if you are referring to a specific skill. Relate answers back to the job for which you are applying. **Behavioral interview questions** are questions that ask candidates to share a past experience related to a workplace situation. An example of a behavioral question is: "Describe a time you motivated others." Prior to answering the question, take a moment to formulate your answer. Use an example that puts you in a positive light and utilizes key skills that are necessary for your target job.

Discrimination and Employee Rights

Title VII of the Civil Rights Act was created to protect the rights of employees. It prohibits employment discrimination based on race, color, religion, sex, or national origin. Other federal laws prohibit pay inequity and discrimination against individuals forty years or older, individuals with disabilities, and individuals who are pregnant. This does not mean that an employer must hire you if you are a minority, pregnant, forty or older, or have a disability. Employers have a legal obligation to provide every qualified candidate equal opportunity to interview. Their job is to hire the most qualified candidate. Unfortunately, some employers ask interview questions that can be discriminatory. Discriminatory questions are illegal. Table 2 was taken from the

Acceptable	Subject	Unacceptable
Table 2	**Illegal Interview Questions**	
Name	**Name**	Maiden name
Place of residence	**Residence**	Questions regarding owning or renting
Statements that employment is subject to verification if applicant meets legal age requirement	**Age**	Age Birth date Date of attendance/completion of school Questions that tend to identify applicants over forty
Statements/inquiries regarding verification of legal right to work in the United States	**Birthplace, citizenship**	Birthplace of applicant or applicant's parents, spouse, or other relatives Requirements that applicant produce naturalization or alien card prior to employment
Languages applicant reads, speaks, or writes if use of language other than English is relevant to the job for which applicant is applying	**National origin**	Questions as to nationality, lineage, ancestry, national origin, descent or parentage of applicant, applicant's spouse, parent, or relative
Statement by employer of regular days, hours, or shifts to be worked	**Religion**	Questions regarding applicant's religion Religious days observed
Name and address of parent or guardian if applicant is a minor. Statement of company policy regarding work assignment of employees who are related	**Sex, marital status, family**	Questions to indicate applicant's sex, marital status, number/ages of children or dependents Questions regarding pregnancy, child birth, or birth control Name/address of relative, spouse, or children of adult applicant
Job-related questions about convictions, except those convictions that have been sealed, expunged, or statutorily eradicated	**Arrest, criminal record**	General questions regarding arrest record

California Department of Fair Employment and Housing to provide examples of acceptable and unacceptable employment inquiries.

If an interviewer asks you a question that is illegal or could be discriminatory, do not directly answer the question; instead, address the issue. For example, if the interviewer states, "You look Hispanic—are you?" Your response should not be "Yes" or "No." Politely smile and say, "People wonder about my ethnicity. What can I tell you about my qualifications for this job?" Also, do not

Role-play an interview. During the interview, ask one legal question and one illegal question. Practice answering the illegal question with confidence but in a non-offensive manner.

accuse the interviewer of asking an illegal question or say, "I will not answer that question because it is illegal." Most employers do not realize they are asking illegal questions. However, some employers purposely ask inappropriate questions. In this case, you need to decide if you want to work for an employer who intentionally asks illegal questions. If employers are behaving inappropriately during an interview, one would wonder how they will treat the applicant after he or she is hired.

Know and protect your rights. It is inappropriate to disclose personal information about yourself during an interview. Avoid making any comment referring to your marital status, children, religion, age, or any other private issue protected by law.

Tough Questions

Life is unpredictable and sometimes results in situations that can be embarrassing or difficult to explain during a job interview. These situations may include a negative work experience with a previous employer, time gaps in a résumé, or a prior felony conviction. The following information provides the proper response to interview questions related to these difficult situations.

Some job seekers have had negative work-related experiences that they do not want to disclose during an interview. Disclosing such information could be potentially devastating to a job interview if it is not handled properly. Some of these experiences include being fired, having a poor performance evaluation, or knowing that a former manager or teacher will not provide a positive reference if called. Perhaps you behaved in a negative manner prior to leaving your old job.

If you did have a difficult circumstance and are not asked about the situation, you have no need to disclose the unpleasant event. The only exception to this rule is if your current or former boss has the potential to provide a negative reference. If this is the situation, tell the interviewer that you know you will not receive a positive reference from him or her and request that the interviewer contact another manager or coworker who will provide a fair assessment of your performance.

Being honest and factual is the best answer to any difficult question. If you were fired, performed poorly, or left in a negative manner, state the facts, but do not go into great detail. Tell the interviewer that you have matured and realize that you did not handle the situation appropriately. Add what lesson you have learned. Do not speak poorly of your current or previous employer, boss, or coworker. It is also important to not place blame by stating who was right or wrong in your negative workplace situation.

It is common for an individual to have time gaps in a résumé as a result of staying at home to raise a young child, care for an elderly relative, or continue his or her education. Those who have gaps in their résumé may need to be prepared to explain what they did during the time gap. Identify a key skill you sharpened during your time gap and relate this experience to a key skill necessary for your target job and industry. For example, if you stayed at home to care for an elderly relative and are asked about the time gap, explain the situation without providing specific details, and then share how the experience improved your time management and organizational skills in addition to improving your awareness of diverse populations including the elderly and disabled.

If you have a felony record, you may be asked about your conviction. As with other difficult interview questions, be honest and factual in your response. Explain the situation, and tell the interviewer that you are making every attempt to start anew and are committed to doing your very best. Sell your strengths, and remember to communicate how your skills will help the company achieve its goals. Your self-confidence and honesty will be revealed through your body language and eye contact. Be sincere. Depending on the type and severity of your offense, it may take more attempts to secure a job than during a typical job search. You may also need to start at a lower level and/or lower pay than desired. The goal is to begin to reestablish credibility. Do not give up. Each experience, be it positive or negative, is a learning experience.

Closing the Interview

After the interviewer has completed his or her questioning, you may be asked if you have any questions. Having a question or closing statement prepared for use at the close of your interview demonstrates to your prospective employer that you have conducted research on the company. A good question refers to a current event that has occurred within the company. For example, "Ms. Dancey, I read about how your company employees donated time to clean up the ABC school yard. Is this an annual event?" A statement such as this provides you one last opportunity to personalize the interview and demonstrate that you researched the company. This is also a good time to share any relevant information you have in your portfolio.

Do not ask questions that imply you did not research the company or that you care only about your needs. Inappropriate questions include questions regarding salary, benefits, or vacations. These questions imply that you care more about what the company can do for you than what you can do for the company. However, it is appropriate to ask what the next steps will be in the interview process, including when a hiring decision will be made.

Questions You *May* Ask the Interviewer

1. Does your company have any plans for expansion?
2. What type of formal training does your company offer?
3. What is the greatest challenge your industry is currently facing?
4. What is the next step in the interview process?
5. What are the required work days and hours of the position?
6. When will you be making a hiring decision?

Questions You *Should Not* Ask During an Interview

1. How much does this job pay?
2. How many sick days do I get?
3. What benefits will I get?
4. What does your company do?
5. How long does it take for someone to get fired for poor performance?

After the interviewer answers your general questions, make a closing interview statement. Restate your personal commercial and ask for the job. An example of a good closing statement is to restate your personal commercial and add: "Once again, thank you for your time, Ms. Dancey. As I stated at the beginning of our meeting, I feel I am qualified for this job based upon my experience, knowledge, and demonstrated leadership. I would like this job and believe I will be an asset to XYZ Company." The purpose of the job interview is to sell you and your skills. A sale is useless if you do not close the sale.

After you make your closing statement, the interviewer will signal that the interview is over. He or she will do this either through conversation or through body language, such as standing up and walking toward the door. Prior to leaving the interview, hand the interviewer your personal business card and ask the interviewer for a business card. You will use this business card for the interview follow-up. As you are handed the card, shake the interviewer's hand using a firm shake and eye contact, and thank him or her for his or her time and state that you look forward to hearing from him or her. Remember to continue communicating confidence, friendliness, and professionalism to every company employee you encounter on your way out of the building.

When you leave the building, retrieve your draft thank-you note. Modify your draft thank-you note to include information that was shared during your interview. Handwrite a personalized thank-you note to each individual who interviewed you. Use your finest handwriting and double-check your spelling and grammar. Refer to the business card(s) you collected for correct name spelling. After you have written your note, hand deliver it to the reception area and ask the receptionist to deliver the notes. Your goal is to make a positive last impression and stand out from the other candidates.

After the Interview

After delivering your thank-you notes, congratulate yourself. If you did your best, you should have no regrets. Prior to leaving the company property, make notes regarding specific information you learned about your prospective job and questions you were asked during the interview. Through the excitement of an interview, you may forget parts of your meeting if you do not immediately write notes. Write down what you did right and areas in which you would like to improve. This is a good time for you to evaluate your impressions of the company and determine if it is a company where you will want to work. This information will be helpful in the future.

Salary Negotiation

Soon after your initial interview, you should hear back from the company. At that point, you may be called in for a second interview or may receive a job offer. A job offer may be contingent upon reference and background checks. This will be a good time to contact the individuals on your reference list to provide them an update on your job search and ensure your references are prepared to respond appropriately to the individual conducting your reference check.

If you are a final candidate for the job, the interviewer may ask you about your salary requirements. In order to negotiate an acceptable salary, first conduct research and compare your research to the salary range that was included in the job announcement. Check job postings and conduct online research to determine local and regional salaries. When conducting your salary research, attempt to match the job description as closely as possible to that of the job for which you are applying. Depending on your experience, start a few thousand dollars higher than your desired starting salary and do not forget to consider your experience and/or lack of experience. Some companies do not offer many benefits but offer higher salaries. Other companies offer lower salaries but better benefits. Weigh these factors when determining your desired salary. Prior to stating your salary requirement, sell your skills. For example, "Ms. Dancey, as I mentioned in my initial interview, I have over five years' experience working in a professional accounting office and an accounting degree; therefore, I feel I should earn between $55,000 and $65,000." If you are offered a salary that is not acceptable, use silence and wait for the interviewer to respond. This minute of silence may encourage the employer to offer a higher salary.

Cory's friend Kenny was invited to a second interview. Prior to the interview, Cory and Kenny prepared for potential questions and situations Kenny might encounter during the interview. In their practice, Cory asked Kenny about his starting salary. Kenny said he did not care; he would just be happy to get a job. Cory reminded Kenny that he needed to sell his skills and go into the interview with a desired target salary. Cory and Kenny then conducted an Internet search of both local and statewide jobs that were similar to the one Kenny wants. Kenny was surprised that starting salaries were much higher than he expected. Fortunately, the next day, when the interviewer asked Kenny about his desired starting salary, Kenny was prepared to answer.

Pre-Employment Tests, Screenings and Medical Exams

Pre-employment tests are assessments that are given to potential employees as a means of determining if the applicant possesses the desired knowledge, skills, or abilities required for the job. Pre-employment tests can be giving during the application process, during the interview process, or prior to receiving a job offer. Some employers require applicants to take online pre-employment tests. Some tests may require lifting, others are skills-based, while others measure listening or logic. Legally, pre-employment tests must be job-related. Depending on the type of test, you may be given the results immediately. In other cases, you may need to wait for the results. If you pass the employment test(s), you will be invited to proceed with the interview process. It is common for employers to have applicants who did not pass a pre-employment test to wait a predetermined period prior to reapplying.

Employers may also conduct pre-employment screenings and medical exams. The most common pre-employment screenings include criminal checks, education verification, driver's license history, security checks, employment checks, credit checks, and reference checks. The number and type of pre-employment screenings performed will be based upon how relevant the check is to the job you will be performing. Legally, employers can require medical exams only after a job offer is made. The exam must be required for all applicants for the same job, and the exam must be job-related. Employers are not allowed to ask disability questions related to pre-employment screenings and medical exams. Common medical exams include vision and strength testing. Employers may also require pre-employment drug tests.

An employer legally cannot conduct these checks without your permission. Most employers will secure your permission in writing when you complete an employment application or when you are a finalist for the position.

When You Are Not Offered the Job

As stated at the beginning of the chapter, a job search is similar to a full-time job. It takes time and can sometimes be discouraging. If you are not called in for an interview or fail to receive a job offer, do not be discouraged.

When you are not invited to interview, evaluate your résumé and cover letter. Check for typographical or grammatical errors. Make sure you have listed important skills that reflect the needs of your target job. Have someone who knows you and your skills—and whom you trust—review your cover letter and résumé. Many times, a fresh perspective will catch obvious errors or opportunities for improvement.

If you are invited to interview but do not receive a job offer, do not be discouraged. Remember to make every experience a learning experience. Sit down and carefully review each step in the interview process and grade yourself. Consider your pre-interview preparation, your interview-day appearance, your interview answers, your ability to interject company research into each interview answer, and your overall attitude. Any area that did not receive an "A" grade is an area poised for improvement.

There are several steps you can take to increase the probability for success in your next interview. Consider your overall appearance. Make sure you convey professionalism. Ensure that your clothes are clean and fit properly. Have a hairstyle that is flattering and well kempt. Check that your fingernails and jewelry are appropriate and do not distract from your personality and job skills.

Mentally review job interview questions that were asked and the responses you provided. Every answer should communicate how your skills will assist the target company in achieving success. Review the amount of company research you conducted. Did you feel amply prepared, or did you simply research the bare minimum? If you felt you did conduct the appropriate amount of research, evaluate whether you fully communicated your research to the interviewer.

Assess your body language and attitude. Stand in front of a mirror and practice your answers to difficult and/or illegal questions. If possible, have a friend videotape you and provide an honest evaluation of your appearance, attitude, and body language. Check for nervous gestures, and keep practicing until you are able to control these nervous habits.

Finally, be honest about your overall performance. Did you ask for the job? Did you immediately send a thank-you note to your interviewer(s)? Sell your skills through your mannerisms, answers, and attitude. Your goal is to stand out above the other candidates.

Workplace Dos and Don'ts

Do tailor your résumé and personal commercial to the needs of your targeted employer	*Don't* have unprofessional introductions on your voice-mail message
Do try to schedule your interview at a time that puts you at an advantage over the other candidates and secure information that better prepares you for the interview	*Don't* make demands with the individual scheduling the interview
Do learn as much as you can about the company, its strategy, and its competition	*Don't* forget to include your research information in your interview answers
Do practice interview questions and formulate answers that highlight your skills and experience	*Don't* show up to an interview unprepared
Do remember that your interview begins the minute you step onto company property	*Don't* let your nerves get the better of you in a job interview
Do know how to handle inappropriate questions that may be discriminatory	*Don't* answer an illegal question. Instead address the issue

Concept Review and Application

Summary of Key Concepts

- Create and modify your personal commercial and adapt it to the requirements of your target job
- Review common interview questions and formulate answers as part of your interview preparation

- Conduct a pre-interview practice to ensure you are prepared the day of the interview
- During your interview, communicate how your knowledge, skills, and abilities will be assets to the company
- Understand the laws that protect employees from discrimination in the interviewing and hiring process
- Be prepared to confidently handle gaps in employment and other difficult interview questions
- Know how to sell yourself and professionally ask for the job at the close of an interview

Key Terms

behavioral interview question

personal commercial

unstructured interview question

group interview

one-on-one interview

positive self-talk

interview portfolio

panel interview

structured interview question

If You Were the Boss

1. What kind of information should you share with your current staff members as they prepare to interview a new employee?
2. How would you handle a prospective employee who disclosed inappropriate information during the job interview?

Video Case Study: Good, Bad, and Ugly

This video addresses improper and proper behavior in a job interview. To view these videos, visit the Student Resources: Professionalism section in www.mystudentsuccesslab.com. Then answer the following questions.

1. Of the three candidates, who was dressed appropriately for the interview and who was not?
2. Name four interview recommendations for Shawn.
3. What interview advice would you give to Kevin?
4. How did Francesca specifically use her interview portfolio and personal commercial during her interview?

Video Case Study: Interview Walk-Through

Pearson Education

This video presents expert advice on how to prepare and what to expect the day of an interview. To view these videos, visit the Student Resources: Professionalism section in www.mystudentsuccesslab.com. Then answer the following questions.

1. Name three activities to perform prior to entering the specific interview location.
2. How specifically should you greet the receptionist?
3. What three activities does the expert recommend you do and what are two activities to avoid while waiting in the reception area?

Video Case Study: Preparing for a Phone Interview

This video presents a phone interview between a job applicant and a potential employer. To view these videos, visit the Student Resources: Professionalism section in www.mystudentsuccesslab.com. Then answer the following questions.

1. What improvements could be made to Kevin's voice mail message?
2. Did Kevin answer his phone appropriately and what kind of impression did he make on Karen Gonzales when he answered the phone?
3. Did Kevin handle the background noise appropriately? Why or why not?
4. How could Kevin have been better prepared for this phone interview?
5. If you were Karen would you call Kevin in for a second interview? Why or why not?

Video Case Study: Pre-Interview Activities

This video presents expert advice regarding activities to conduct before the day of an interview. To view these videos, visit the Student Resources: Professionalism section in www.mystudentsuccesslab.com. Then answer the following questions.

1. What scheduling strategy should you utilize when invited to an interview?
2. Name four specific items to be included in an interview portfolio and explain the purpose of each.
3. Name four specific activities that need to take place in preparing your interview outfit.
4. Why is it important to visit the interview site prior to the day of an interview?

Video Case Study: Tough Interview Questions

This video presents expert advice on how to respond to tough interview questions. To view these videos, visit the Student Resources: Professionalism section in www.mystudentsuccesslab.com. Then answer the following questions.

Pearson Education

1. How does the expert recommend you prepare for a tough interview question?
2. What specific advice does the expert share on how to respond to a tough interview question?
3. Provide specific information the expert shared on how to deal with illegal interview questions.

Web Links

http://www.onetcenter.org/
http://jobstar.org/electra/question/sal-req.cfm
http://www.collegegrad.com/intv
http://www.careercc.com/interv3.shtml
http://interview.monster.com
http://www.rileyguide.com/interview.html

Activities

Activity 1

Identify a local company for which you would like to interview. Using the following table, conduct a thorough targeted job search on this company. Answer as many of the questions as possible.

1.	Company name	
2.	Company address	
3.	Job title	
4.	To whom should the cover letter be addressed?	
5.	What are the job requirements?	
6.	Is this a full-time or part-time job?	
7.	What are the hours/days of work?	
8.	What are the working conditions?	
9.	Is there room for advancement?	
10.	What kind of training is offered?	
11.	What other positions at this company match my qualifications?	
12.	What are the average starting salaries (benefits)?	
13.	Is traveling or relocation required?	
14.	Where is the business located (home office, other offices)?	
15.	What are the products or services that the employer provides or manufactures?	
16.	What is the mission statement?	
17.	What kind of reputation does this organization have?	
18.	What is the size of the employer's organization relative to the industry?	
19.	What is the growth history of the organization for the past five, ten, or fifteen years?	
20.	How long has the employer been in business?	
21.	Who is the employer's competition?	

Activity 2

Write a statement to use during an invitation to an interview that will help you secure all relevant interview information.

_____

_____

Activity 3

Using information obtained in your target company research (Activity 1), write three common interview questions and answers. Integrate relevant company information in your answers.

Question	Answer
1.	
2.	
3.	

Activity 4

Conduct a salary search for a target job. Identify the salary range. Using your research data, write out a statement you could use to negotiate a higher salary.

Lowest Salary	Highest Salary
$	$

Salary Negotiation Statement

_____

_____

1. The purpose of a/an _____ is to identify _____ and identify companies for which you would like to work.

2. In addition to finding out with whom you will be interviewing, identify how much _____ _____ the company has scheduled and _____ are being called in to _____.

3. Prior to your interview, _____.

4. If possible, prior to the interview day, _____.

5. When asked a difficult question, be _____ and _____.

Suggested Readings

"How to Stand Out from the Crowd and Kick-Start Your Own Recovery," *U.S. News & World Report* 147 (May 2010): 14–16.

National Association of Colleges and Employers, Bethlehem, PA, www.Jobweb.com

Skorkin, A. The Main Reason Why You Suck at Interviews: Lack of Preparation. *Lifehacker.com*, http://lifehacker.com/5710712/the-main-reason-why-you-suck-at-interviews-lack-of-preparation December 10, 2010.

Garrison, S., Gutter, M., and Spence, L. Managing in Tough Times: Building Your Assets by Volunteering. Department of Family, Youth and Community Sciences, Florida Cooperative Extension Service, Institute of Food and Agricultural Sciences, University of Florida. October 2009, http://edis.ifas.ufl.edu/fy1107#FOOTNOTE_1

Etiquette/Dress

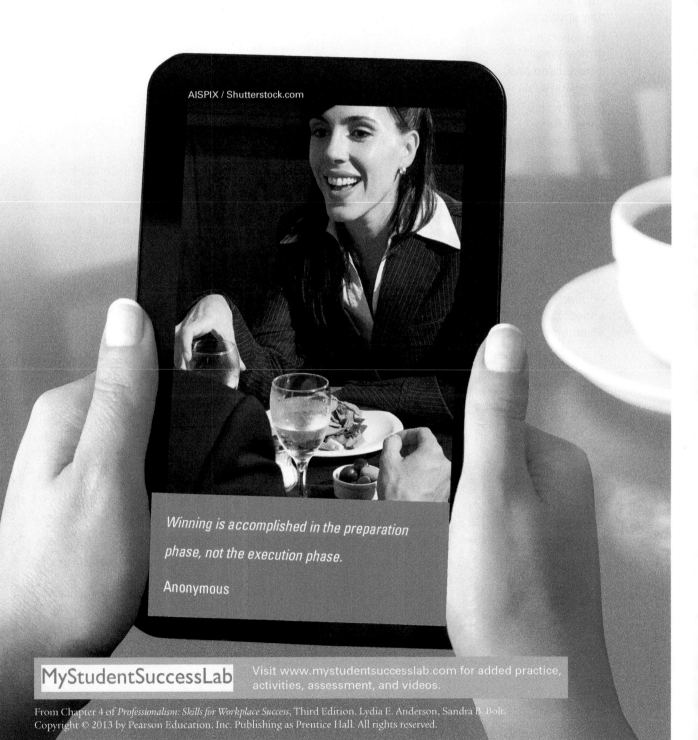

AISPIX / Shutterstock.com

Winning is accomplished in the preparation phase, not the execution phase.

Anonymous

From Chapter 4 of *Professionalism: Skills for Workplace Success*, Third Edition. Lydia E. Anderson, Sandra B. Bolt.

Objectives

- Describe and discuss the importance of professional behavior
- State the impact dress can have on others' perception of you
- Demonstrate a professional introduction and handshake
- Demonstrate appropriate professional behavior in business dining situations
- Recognize and apply the appropriate use of technology in business/social situations
- Utilize professional *etiquette* in appropriate business situations

How-Do-You-Rate

	How proper are you?	True	False
1.	You do not have to shake someone's hand if you already know the person.	❏	❏
2.	Visible tattoos, nose rings, or lip rings, if tasteful, are now acceptable in a professional business situation.	❏	❏
3.	If you are invited to a business meal, you may order anything on the menu.	❏	❏
4.	Sending a handwritten thank-you note is no longer necessary.	❏	❏
5.	It is now acceptable business practice to read a text message during business meetings.	❏	❏

If you answered "true" to two or more of these questions, it is time to begin actively practicing business etiquette. While business protocol may vary in some industries, it is best to lean toward a conservative, traditional approach until you are confident of acceptable industry standards.

Executive Presence

Employees represent their company. Therefore, the way you communicate, dress, and behave, both inside and outside the company, contributes to others' perception of you and your company. Consistently demonstrating proper etiquette and protocol in business, dining, and social situations results in positive business relationships. The way you look and behave is a reflection of the organization for which you work. **Executive presence** is defined as having the attitude of an executive. Projecting an executive presence demonstrates to employers that they have hired a new employee with knowledge regarding appropriate workplace behavior.

Many of our parents taught us early in life that good manners, such as smiling and saying please and thank you in social situations, create positive relationships. Those successful at work understand the basics regarding expected professional behavior on topics including attire, business protocol, social etiquette, dining, and the appropriate use of technology. You will encounter many social situations at work. Knowing how to behave in professional social situations will help you be more successful in workplace relationships. Some of this information may be new to you, and you may feel awkward when you first implement these positive behaviors. The purpose of this chapter is to prepare you for many of the social experiences you will face in the workplace.

Influences of Dress in a Professional Environment

Both your maturity and the importance you place on your job are reflected in the way you behave and dress at work. Because impressions are often made in the first few minutes of meeting someone, individuals rarely have time to even speak before an impression is formed. The majority of first impressions are made through visual **appearance,** which is how you look. Coworkers, bosses, and customers form attitudes based on appearance. Appearance also has an impact on how you perform at work. If you dress professionally, you are more apt to act in a professional manner. The more casually you dress, the more casually you tend to behave. Think of your appearance as a frame. A frame is used to highlight a picture. You do not want the frame to be too fancy, because it will take away from the picture. You want a frame to complement the picture. The frame highlights not only your physical features, including your face, but also your attitude, knowledge, and potential.

Exercise 1   Define Your "Frame"

What does your frame look like? Be honest.

Is it trendy, outdated, professional, or inconsistent?

_____

Does it complement your desired appearance as a professional?

_____

If your current frame is not yet professional, what changes need to occur?

_____

_____

One of the toughest transitions to make when entering the workplace is choosing appropriate dress. Dressing professionally does not have to conflict with current fashion trends. The trick is to know what is acceptable. A basic rule of thumb is to dress one position higher than your current position (i.e., dress like your boss). Doing so communicates that you are serious about your career and how you represent the company. Dressing professionally will assist you in projecting a favorable image at work and position you for job advancement.

Know your workplace dress policies, and understand that professional dress carries different meaning depending on both the industry and work environment. One of the first steps to determining appropriate attire for work is to identify your company's **dress code.** A dress code is a policy that addresses issues such as required attire, uniforms, hairstyle, undergarments, jewelry, and shoes. Dress codes vary by company depending on the industry, the specific work area, and health/safety issues. If your company has a mandatory uniform, the company dress code will be detailed. If a uniform is not required, identify what is and is not acceptable attire by reading the dress code policy, by observing what is practiced in the workplace, or by asking your supervisor. Some dress codes are vague, while others are specific. Work attire should pose no safety hazards. Unstable footwear that does not provide protection are not appropriate. Dangling jewelry that could be caught in equipment is also inappropriate for work. As previously stated, organizational dress policies exist for customer service, safety, and security reasons. Frequently, these policies are included in the employee handbook. If there is no policy, ask your boss if there is a formal dress code and secure a copy. An important cue to workplace attire is to observe how managers dress. Suits are not always the preferred attire in an office environment. In some situations, pants are acceptable for women, while in other situations they are not. Note that sweats (shirts and/or pants) are not appropriate for the traditional workplace.

Once you have identified what your organization considers proper attire, begin to create a **work wardrobe.** These are clothes that you primarily wear only to work and work-related functions. You need not invest a lot of money when building a work wardrobe. Start with basic pieces and think conservative. For women working in a traditional office environment, this attire includes a simple, solid skirt or pantsuit in a dark color and a blazer. Skirt length should not be above the knee. Pants should be worn with a matching blazer. For most office environments, men should select dark slacks, a matching jacket, and a tie. If you are just starting your job and cannot afford new clothing, these items can sometimes be found inexpensively at thrift and discount stores. If these items are purchased at a thrift store, inspect them for tears or stains and take them to the dry cleaner for cleaning and pressing. You will be surprised how professional these items look after they are cleaned and pressed. Select items that are made of quality fabrics that will not wear out quickly, fit properly, and are comfortable. As you begin to earn money, continue building your wardrobe and develop a style that conforms to both company policy and your taste.

Casual Workdays and Special Events

Many companies allow **casual workdays.** These are days when companies relax their dress code. Unfortunately, some employees attempt to stretch the term casual. If your company has a casual workday, remember that you are still at work and should dress appropriately. Of course, you can wear jeans if jeans are the preferred attire; just adhere to the head-to-toe tips presented later in this chapter. Do not wear clothing that is tattered, stained, or torn (even if it is considered stylish). Avoid wearing shirts with sayings or graphics that may offend others. In general, it is best to dress modestly.

As you learn more about professional dress and expectations regarding professional attire, consider cultural and geographic differences and expectations. Globally, differing cultural expectations apply to workplace dress. In some countries, women must be completely covered from head to toe, while in other countries, women should not wear pants. "Business casual" for men on the East Coast of the United States may require a suit jacket, while "business casual" on the West Coast of the United States may allow for wearing khaki pants and a polo shirt. When conducting business in a geographic area different than yours (whether in your own country or abroad), research appropriate attire prior to your visit.

Your company may also host or invite you to attend a special function. Holiday parties and receptions are examples. In these situations, instead of daily work attire, more formal attire may be required. Just as with casual workdays, stick with the basics provided in the head-to-toe tips. Women, if appropriate, should wear something in a more formal fabric. Although you have increased freedom and flexibility regarding style and length, this is still a work-related function, so dress conservatively and not suggestively. Men, check ahead of time and see if tuxedos are preferred. For most semiformal occasions, a suit will suffice.

As a reward for being selected Employee of the Month, Cory was invited to attend a one-day conference luncheon with several managers from the company. Cory had not attended a function like this before and was a little nervous about how to dress and behave in this new business situation. Cory did some preparation and found that dress and behavior are as important in public situations as they are at work. Cory checked with others who had attended these functions and decided that dressing in formal business attire would be most appropriate. Cory made sure to shower, clean and trim fingernails, wear polished shoes, and not wear inappropriate jewelry. When entering the conference, Cory was glad to have conducted research, as nearly everyone was dressed in formal business attire.

Talk It Out

Identify people in class who are wearing something appropriate for a casual workday.

Tips from Head to Toe

Regardless of the company's dress code, practice these basic hygiene rules:

- *Shower daily.* If needed, use deodorant. Use perfume, lotion, or cologne sparingly. Scent should not be overpowering.
- *Clothes should be clean and ironed, not torn or tattered, and should fit properly.*
- *Hair should be clean, well kempt, and a natural color.* Your hairstyle should reflect your profession. Fad hairstyles and unnatural color are inappropriate in many workplaces.
- *Practice good dental hygiene.* Brushing and flossing your teeth both in the morning and at bedtime, if not more often, not only ensures clean teeth and fresh breath, it also helps prevent tooth decay. Many public health clinics provide no-cost or low-cost dental care.
- *Hands and nails should be clean, well groomed, and trimmed.* Unnaturally long nails are inappropriate. Polish or artwork if allowed, should be neat and kept conservative.
- *Jewelry should be kept to a minimum.* Jewelry should complement your outfit. Do not wear anything that is distracting or makes noise.
- *Shoes should be in good condition.* Keep shoes polished and free of scuffs. Flip-flops are not appropriate for the workplace. Men's sock color should match shoe or pant color. Women, keep heels in good condition; repair or replace them as needed. Heels should not be too high. Nylons should be free of runs and snags.

A woman's outfit should reflect her style and personality—within reason. When dressing for work, your goal is to appropriately frame yourself in a manner that draws attention to your professional qualities (i.e., your brains and inner beauty). Additional tips for women include the following:

- *Makeup should be for day wear.* Makeup is appropriate for work. Makeup that makes people think you are going to a bar after work is not. Do not wear heavy eyeliner, eyeshadow in colors that draw attention, or lipstick in bold colors.
- *It is not acceptable to wear suggestive clothing.* Visible cleavage or bare midriffs are inappropriate for work. No matter the current fashion trends, undergarments (bras and panties) should not be visible. Skirts worn at work should be no shorter than knee length.

Just like a woman's outfit, a man's outfit should reflect his style and personality. For some positions, a suit may not be appropriate. The biggest wardrobe blunder men make is wearing clothing that is not clean and/or pressed. After checking your company's dress code, heed these unspoken rules regarding professional dress at work for men:

- *Shave and/or trim facial hair, including nose and ear hair.*
- *In an office environment, dress pants are the only pants that are professional.* With the exception of casual workdays, jeans are inappropriate. Baggy pants that reveal underwear are also inappropriate. Whenever possible, wear a neutral, plain belt that does not draw attention.
- *Shirts should be tucked in.* A polo shirt or a dress shirt with a tie is best. Shirts should not display excessive wear (check around the collar line for fraying or stains). Shirts with offensive logos or offensive phrases are inappropriate at work.
- *Hats should not be worn inside buildings except for religious purposes.*

Talk It Out

When or when not is it appropriate for a woman to be sleeveless in a professional setting?

Jewelry, Body Piercing, and Tattoos

As with professional attire, you do not want to wear or display anything that brings unwanted attention to you in the workplace. While body art and piercings are becoming more common and acceptable in society, many companies have policies that prohibit visible tattoos and/or visible body piercings beyond one in each ear. Body art and piercings are offensive to some individuals. Many people get a tattoo and/or body piercing to signify a special event, individual, or symbol. If you are considering getting a tattoo or body piercing, consider the long-term consequences of doing so. Relationships and situations change. Tattoos and some piercings are difficult and painful, if not impossible, to remove. While you may currently not care how society feels about your tattoo and/or piercing, you may regret your decision in the future. If you already have body art and/or piercing, it is recommended that you cover your tattoo with clothing, makeup, or other means until you are clear on your employer's policy regarding visible body art. Many companies also have strict policies on body piercings beyond earrings. Some piercings close quickly, so it may be impossible to remove the piercing during work hours. Other forms of piercings, such as microdermal piercings, cannot be easily removed. In these cases, determine which is more important—a job, or your body art and/or piercing. In general, follow these guidelines regarding jewelry, piercings, and tattoos:

- Nose rings, lip rings, and/or tongue rings are not professional and should not be worn in a professional setting. Any other body piercing/body jewelry should not be visible at work.
- More than two earrings worn on each ear is considered unprofessional.
- Earrings, chains, and other jewelry should not draw attention. This includes symbols or words that could be considered offensive to others.
- Body art (tattoos) should not be visible at work.

Business Etiquette

In a modern workplace, human interaction is unavoidable. Our society has a standard of social behavior that is called **etiquette.** Typically, when individuals think of etiquette, they think it applies only to high society. This is not true. Socially acceptable behavior should penetrate all demographic and economic groups. Individuals wanting to succeed in the workplace need to heed this protocol and consistently utilize proper etiquette not only at work, but in all areas of their life.

Before we study common areas of business etiquette, we need to define a few terms. Understanding these terms and integrating them into your daily routine will make it much easier to carry out the desired and appropriate workplace behavior. The first word is **courtesy.** When you display courtesy, you are exercising manners, respect, and consideration toward others. The second word is **respect.** Respect is defined as holding someone in high regard. This means putting others' needs before your own needs. Displaying both courtesy and respect toward others are the keys in becoming ladies and gentlemen at work.

Some of the first words most parents teach young children are *please* and *thank you.* Although they are not used as frequently as they should be, both are extremely valuable terms that can actually create power for you at work. Think about it; when someone says "please" and "thank you" to you, you are more likely to repeat a favor or gesture because your deed was acknowledged. When someone does something nice, verbally say "thank you." Not doing so makes you appear selfish and unappreciative. When you express thanks, individuals will be more likely to continue performing kind acts for you.

Make it a habit to write a thank-you note when someone does something for you that takes more than five minutes or when someone gives you a gift. Write the note as soon as possible. Do not wait more than three days to write the thank-you note.

Talk It Out

Discuss ways you can be courteous and respectful in class.

Handshakes

A good handshake conveys confidence. Make a habit of greeting others in business situations with a professional handshake and friendly verbal greeting. Approach the individual you are greeting, make eye contact, smile, and extend your right hand as you verbalize a greeting. For example, "Hello Ms. Cao, my name is Talia. We met at last week's meeting. It's nice to see you again." Ms. Cao will extend her right hand. Your two hands should meet at the web (see Figure 1). Grip the other person's hand and gently squeeze and shake hands.

- Do not squeeze the other hand too firmly.
- Shake the entire hand and not just the other person's fingers. Doing so is insulting and implies that you feel you are better than the other person.
- Do not place your hand on top of the other person's hand or pat the hand. Doing so is insulting.
- If your palms are sweaty, discretely wipe your palm on the side of your hip prior to shaking.

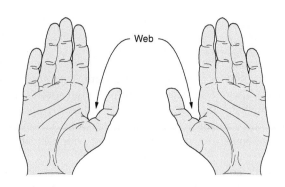

Web

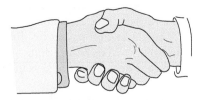

Figure 1

Proper Handshake

A good handshake takes practice. As mentioned earlier, get into the habit of being the first to greet and introduce yourself to others. At first you may not feel comfortable, but practice makes perfect. The more frequently you initiate a good handshake, the more comfortable and confident you will become.

Exercise 2   Shake Hands

With another person practice initiating an introduction, making sure to include a professional handshake. Rate the quality of the introduction and handshake on a scale of 1 to 5, with 5 being the best. Discuss what improvements should be made.

Introductions and Business Networking

An element of success in the workplace involves meeting new people. This process of meeting and developing relationships with individuals outside of one's immediate work area is referred to as **networking.** Networking is also commonly used in the job search process. In the workplace, creating a professional network is a useful tool for collaboration. In a business situation when you do not know someone in the room, increase your confidence by being the first to initiate a conversation. After you have introduced yourself, ask your new acquaintance about himself or herself. Learn about his or her job and find something you have in common. Keep the initial conversation focused on him or her. Your goal is to meet new people and create a positive impression so that if you see them again or contact them in the future, they will remember and have a favorable impression of you.

At times, you will be with individuals who do not know each other. When you are with two people who do not know each other and you know both people, it is your responsibility to introduce the two individuals to each other. Politely introduce the lower-ranking person to the higher-ranking person. For example, "Matt, this is Ryan McClaine, the president of our company." "Ryan, this is Matt Yu, my next-door neighbor." Apply this introduction rule to all social situations, including dining, meetings, receptions, and parties. Making introductions to others is an excellent form of networking. After you have introduced the two individuals, if possible, provide a piece of information about one of the individuals that creates a foundation for a conversation. For example, "Ryan, you and Matt attended the same college."

Appointments

A daily function of business is making and keeping appointments. Appointments can occur in many forms, such as face-to-face meetings, over the phone, or through current technologies (e-mail, texting, or video chat). When setting meeting times, check regional time differences and clearly include the regional time zone abbreviation in your confirmation if you are located in different time zones. For example, "I look forward to meeting with you on Tuesday, April 21st, at 9 a.m. Pacific Standard Time (PST)."

Sometimes you will be required to work with receptionists and/or administrative assistants to schedule appointments. Be kind to the receptionist and/or administrative assistant. These individuals are the gatekeepers to their bosses; they control schedules and often wield great power in decisions. When scheduling an appointment, state your name, the purpose, and the desired date and time of the meeting. If possible, avoid scheduling appointments on Monday mornings; many people use Monday mornings to schedule their own week and are less likely to accommodate you. If you will be arriving late to an appointment, call and let the other party know you are running late. If you must cancel an appointment, do so immediately and apologize for any inconvenience. Do not just ignore an appointment.

If your meeting is to take place on the telephone, ensure you are holding the call in a quiet place where you will not have distracting background noise. Use a reliable phone connection. If your meeting requires Internet technologies, use a reliable connection and log in at least ten minutes early to ensure a proper connection. If your meeting involves video chat with a web camera, dress professionally and hold your meeting in a professional location. In general, an office or study is most appropriate. Due to confidentiality issues, problems with noise, and the need for a professional backdrop, do not use a public location.

When keeping an appointment (face-to-face or via technology), arrive or check in five minutes early. For face-to-face meetings, after you enter the office, greet the receptionist and politely introduce yourself. State whom you have an appointment with and the time of the meeting. When entering an office for a meeting, wait to be invited to sit down. At the close of any meeting, thank the other participants for their time. If you are in person, exchange business cards if appropriate and close with a final handshake. .

Dining

In the workplace, you will encounter a variety of dining situations. Some dining experiences will be less formal than others. You will most likely come across some form of the table setting illustrated in Figure 2. Take time to study and review a common place setting to learn the proper location and use for utensils, plates, and cups. Apart from fast food, few college students are generally comfortable eating in a formal dining situation. Here are several rules of thumb regarding dining etiquette:

- As soon are you are seated, place your napkin on your lap. If you leave the table, place your napkin to the side of your plate, not on your chair.
- Do not discuss business matters until everyone has ordered. Table conversation should be positive and free of controversial subjects such as politics and religion.
- Utensils are set to be used in order of necessity. As your courses are served, start with the outside utensil and work in, toward the plate. The utensils set at the top of the plate are for your dessert.
- When serving coffee, water, tea, or any other beverage available at the table, first offer and serve others at your table.
- Do not order anything expensive or messy.
- Do not order alcohol unless others at your table first order an alcoholic beverage. Abstaining from alcohol is the most desired behavior. If you choose to drink, limit consumption to one drink.
- When bread is available, first offer bread to others at your table before taking a piece.

1	napkin
2	plate
3	salad fork
4	dinner fork
5	dinner knife
6	teaspoon
7	soup spoon
8	salad plate
9	bread plate
10	butter knife
11	dessert spoon
12	dessert fork
13	water glass
14	beverage/wine glass
15	coffee cup and saucer

Figure 2

Table Setting

- Place your bread on the bread plate (located at the top left corner of your dinner plate). Place your serving of butter on the bread plate. Do not butter the entire piece of bread at one time. Tear a piece of bread and butter only that piece of bread before eating.
- Do not take the last piece of bread or appetizer unless it is first offered to others at your table.
- When your meal arrives, do not begin eating until everyone at your table has been served. If everyone receives their meals except you (you are the last to be served), give others at your table permission to begin eating without you so that their food does not get cold. Eat your meal at the same pace as others at the table.
- Do not eat your meal with your fingers unless your main course is meant to be eaten without utensils.
- Be kind and polite to the staff and servers.
- Burping and slurping are inappropriate while dining. If you accidentally burp or slurp, immediately apologize and say "excuse me." Also, chew with your mouth closed.
- When you are finished eating, place your knife and fork together, with the blade facing in and the tines up. When you are only resting and you do not want the server to take your plate away, cross your utensils with the tines facing down.
- It is inappropriate to use a mobile communication device while dining. If you must take a call or text, excuse yourself from the table.

When Cory arrived at the conference, Cory was glad to be dressed professionally. Everyone was dressed in business attire. As Cory was introduced to others, Cory was sure to make eye contact, smile, and properly shake hands. Cory also collected many business cards while networking. During the meal, Cory was careful to follow dining etiquette. At work the next day, Cory immediately wrote a thank-you note to the managers who invited Cory to the event. At the end of the day, Cory's manager called Cory and let Cory know what a great impression Cory made at the conference. Several colleagues had mentioned to Cory's manager how impressed they were with Cory's professionalism. Cory realized that conducting a little research and being professional was well worth the effort.

A common activity in business involves attending social functions. Many invitations request an RSVP, which is French for *répondez s'il vous plaît* (i.e., please respond). As soon as you receive an invitation, send a reply—whether it is an acceptance to attend or a regret that you cannot attend. Not acknowledging the invitation and failing to respond is rude.

When you attend a social function, remember that you are attending it to meet and network with other professionals. Do not focus on the food; focus on the networking opportunities.

- As with dining situations, refrain from or limit the consumption of alcohol.
- If you choose to eat, serve yourself a small plate of hors d'oeuvres and move away from the food table.
- Hold your hors d'oeuvres in your left hand, leaving your right hand free to shake hands and greet others.
- If there are name badges, wear one placed neatly on your right shoulder. If you must handwrite your own name badge, print your first and last name clearly.
- Do not talk with food in your mouth.

Talk It Out

Share common dining and social situations that make you uncomfortable, and identify how best to deal with these situations.

Web Quiz

Rate your workplace etiquette. Use the following website, or find another etiquette web quiz.

http://www.usatoday. com/img/content/flash/ getiquettequiz/flash.htm

Other Etiquette Basics

At first glance, business etiquette can be a bit overwhelming. However, with practice, business etiquette becomes habit. When in doubt, mimic what the most polished person in the room is doing. Be aware of your surroundings and watch and learn from those whom you admire. The following is a final list of etiquette tips to assist you in becoming one of the most admired and respected individuals in the workplace.

- *Have a pleasant attitude.* In addition to saying "please" and "thank you," do not underestimate the value of a simple smile and eye contact. If you have a positive attitude, it will be reflected in your demeanor. When encountering people in the hallways, elevators, and/or meeting rooms, smile, make eye contact, and greet them.
- *Knock before entering an office.* Do not enter an office or private workspace such as a cubicle until you are invited. If the individual you want to see normally has his or her door open, do not disturb the individual when the door is closed. The exception is for an emergency or urgent situation needing his or her attention—but apologize for interrupting. If the door is open but the individual is with someone else, politely wait your turn.
- *Put others first.* When you are with colleagues and you are taking turns (in line, to order, etc.), allow your colleagues to go first. Doing so shows respect and courtesy.
- *Apologize when necessary.* Everyone is human. Therefore, everyone makes mistakes. When you realize that you may have said or done something hurtful to someone, apologize immediately. Apologizing is not a sign of weakness. Apologizing is a sign of strength and maturity. Even if you are not certain if you have offended someone, apologize to avoid any potential misunderstandings. However, do not unnecessarily and continually apologize. Doing so not only gives you the appearance of being needy and insecure, more importantly you are not being assertive and possibly not standing up for your rights in an unoffending manner.
- *Do not use profanity.* The use of profanity is not appropriate in the workplace. Even if others in your presence use profanity, do not assume everyone is comfortable with the bad language. Conversations should be professional, respectful, and free of profanity.
- *Avoid dominating a conversation.* There is a key to carrying on a successful conversation: listening. When you are an active listener, you value the information the other individual is providing. Too frequently, individuals dominate a conversation with their own personal accounts. In general, this is not appropriate. This behavior becomes annoying to the listener when you turn the conversation to yourself. Next time you are in a conversation, listen to how many times you state the words *me, I,* and *my.* Try to minimize the use of these words in your conversation.

Workplace Dos and Don'ts

Do wear professional clothes to work	*Don't* wear sweats, flip flops, or suggestive apparel at work
Do shower and make sure you are always clean	*Don't* overdo the cologne (or any body sprays)
Do make eye contact and offer a gentle but firm handshake	*Don't* grasp just the fingers when shaking hands
Do follow formal dining etiquette at work-related functions	*Don't* reach, grab, or overload your plate at the hors d'oeuvres table
Do say "please" and "thank you" when appropriate	*Don't* assume that the other person knows you are thankful for his or her act of kindness

Concept Review and Application

Summary of Key Concepts

- Projecting an executive presence is important in demonstrating knowledge of basic workplace behavior
- The majority of first impressions are made through visual appearances
- Both your maturity and the importance you place on your job are reflected in the way you behave and dress at work
- Begin to create a work wardrobe today
- Visual body art/piercing and body rings/jewelry are offensive to some individuals and are not appropriate in a professional work environment. Consider the long-term consequences of getting a tattoo or piercing
- Follow business etiquette protocol and consistently utilize it in all areas of your life
- Make a habit of thanking individuals either verbally or in writing
- Appropriate etiquette at social functions and while dining is as important as professional behavior at work

Key Terms

appearance	casual workdays	courtesy
dress code	etiquette	executive presence
networking	respect	work wardrobe

If You Were the Boss

1. You are the manager of a bank, and one of your employees comes in on a Monday morning with a pierced tongue and purple hair. What should you do?
2. You have just hired a new employee who clearly has no concept of business etiquette. What specific steps would you take to teach your new employee how to behave professionally?

Video Case Study: Dress for Success

This video presents expert advice on how to dress professionally at work. To view these videos, visit the Student Resources: Professionalism section in www.mystudentsuccesslab.com. Then answer the following questions:

1. What specifically are Francesca and Brad wearing that makes their appearance professional?
2. What four items make Patricia's and Brian's appearance unprofessional?
3. What specific advice does the expert provide for looking professional regarding makeup, tattoos, jewelry, jeans, hair, and shoes?

Video Case Study: Business Lunch Etiquette

Pearson Education

This video addresses a common business lunch sales meeting. To view these videos, visit the Student Resources: Professionalism section in www.mystudentsuccesslab.com. Then answer the following questions:

1. Name three things Brian did right or wrong.
2. What advice would you give Brian?
3. Midway through this lunch, how should Karen have handled this situation?

Web Links

http://www.ravenwerks.com/practices/etiquette.htm

Activities

Activity 1

Assume you are starting a new job as an accounting clerk next week. You need a work wardrobe and are limited to a $50 budget. Make a list of what you need and could buy to get you through your first week of work. Include the cost.

What You Need to Buy	Cost
	$
Total Cost	$50

Prior to being faced with this scenario, what items can you purchase today to begin building your professional wardrobe?

Activity 2

Imagine you are at a business reception and you do not know anyone else in the room. Role-play formal introductions with a classmate, and then evaluate your partner's performance by identifying strengths and weaknesses.

STUDENT NAME	
Strengths	Weaknesses

STUDENT NAME	
Strengths	Weaknesses

Activity 3

Visit a (non-fast-food) restaurant to practice proper dining etiquette. While you are doing so, identify five acts of inappropriate behavior others are exhibiting and explain why this behavior is not professional.

Inappropriate Behavior	Why Behavior Is Not Professional
1.	
2.	
3.	
4.	
5.	

1. The majority of first impressions are made by _____.

2. One of the first steps to determining appropriate attire for work is to identify

   _____.

3. Provide five tips for women for dressing professionally from head to toe.

   _____, _____, _____,

   _____,_____.

4. Provide five tips for men for dressing professionally from head to toe.

   _____,

   _____, _____, _____,

   _____.

5. A standard of social behavior is called _____.

6. When someone does something nice for you, you should _____.

7. A good handshake conveys _____.

8. Provide five rules of thumb regarding dining etiquette. _____,

   _____, _____, _____,

   _____.

Suggested Readings

The Emily Post Institute, Burlington, VT, www.emilypost.com

Wayne, T. "Why Etiquette Schools Are Thriving," *Bloomberg Business Week* (October 14, 2010).

Fisher, A. "Is Cubical Etiquette an Oxymoron?" *CNNMoney* (October 22, 2010).

McAfee, A. "Mistakes Millennials Make at Work," *Harvard Business Review* (August 30, 2010).

"Discovering Hats, a New Generation Brims with Anxiety Over Etiquette," *Wall Street Journal* (August 11, 2010).

Schrage, M. "Why Your Looks Will Matter More," *Harvard Business Review* (April 22, 2010).

Tillotson, K. "Manners Mean More in Tough Job Market," *Minneapolis Star Tribune* (March 22, 2010).

Career Changes

olly / Shutterstock.com

Real success is finding your lifework in the work that you love.

David McCullough (b. 1933)

MyStudentSuccessLab Visit www.mystudentsuccesslab.com for added practice, activities, assessment, and videos.

From Chapter 16 of *Professionalism: Skills for Workplace Success*, Third Edition. Lydia E. Anderson, Sandra B. Bolt.

Objectives

- Explain the importance of *training* and *development*
- Define the importance of continual *formal learning* and *informal learning*
- Know the various ways employment status can change
- Define the various types of workplace terminations
- Demonstrate how to write a *letter of resignation*
- Know the appropriate behavior to exhibit when leaving a position
- Understand the opportunities of becoming an *entrepreneur*

How-Do-You-Rate

	Do you understand job transition?	True	False
1.	It is normal to change jobs within the same company.	❑	❑
2.	Being fired is not the same as being laid off.	❑	❑
3.	It is appropriate to look for a new job while still employed.	❑	❑
4.	With the exception of being fired, when leaving a job, an employee should always write a thank-you note to his or her former boss.	❑	❑
5.	Many people start their own business if they are unable to find a job.	❑	❑

If you answered "true" to the majority of these questions, well done. You are aware of important concepts related to career and life changes.

Career Changes

Where do you want to be in five years? While this is a common interview question, it is also part of goal setting. Career changes should be welcome, because they mean you are accomplishing and updating your goals. Career changes are normal and common occurrences. While most of these changes can be controlled, some career changes are unexpected. Make a commitment to become a lifelong learner so you have current knowledge and skills to deal with unexpected change. This chapter explores the various career changes that may occur and teaches you how to welcome change as an opportunity for both personal and career growth.

Training and Development

Many companies offer current and new employees **training** to learn new skills. The teaching of new skills may be used to promote employees and/or increase their responsibilities. With the increase of technology usage, employee training is important for many companies. Training is usually provided and/or paid for by the company.

In addition to learning new skills through training, make every effort to attend **development** sessions designed to enhance existing skills or increase your skills. Development sessions make employees more diverse in knowledge, skills, and abilities, which provides an advantage when promotional or other opportunities arise in the workplace. Even if you do not think a development session is in your area of expertise, continue expanding your knowledge and skills in as many areas as possible. This is especially helpful if you are considering a promotion into a management position.

As an employee who is considering a management position, learn not only the skills needed for your job, but also other skills. Be aware of the key duties within other departments. The development of these skills will increase your knowledge and understanding of the company's mission and goals. When you can see beyond your job, you become more aware of what you are contributing to the company and how you are helping make it more successful.

The marketing department for Cory's company invited all employees to meet in the conference room during lunch hour to learn more about how to conduct a media interview. Cory did not know a lot about marketing and did not think media interviews were a part of Cory's job. However, Cory attended because it would be not only a good skill to learn, but also a good way to meet people in other departments.

Continual Learning

In addition to training and development programs offered by a company, there are other ways to improve and increase your skills and knowledge. **Continual learning** is the ongoing process of increasing knowledge in the area of your career. This can be accomplished by formal and/or informal learning.

Formal learning involves returning to college to increase knowledge, improve skills, or receive an additional or advanced degree. This can be done while you continue working. Consider taking one or two night classes a semester while you work. Be cautious about taking too many classes while working full-time, because that might stress you to a point that you will perform poorly at both work and school. Many colleges offer online classes, which have become increasingly popular for working adults. These classes allow more freedom and flexibility by allowing students to complete coursework on the Internet.

In addition to college, seminars and conferences are available. Some of these seminars and conferences offer college credit. Many seminars and conferences are offered by vendors or industry experts. Although you may have to pay for a conference, your company may be willing to reimburse you or share the cost with you. Conferences may last one day or may take place over a period of several days. Seminars and conferences are also excellent methods of expanding your professional network.

Informal learning is increasing knowledge by reading career-related magazines, newsletters, and electronic articles associated with your job. Another means of informal learning is using the Internet to research career-related information. Informal learning is an ongoing process and can occur during informational interviews, in conversations with professionals in your career area, and by attending association meetings. Make every opportunity a learning opportunity.

Talk It Out

Based on your target career, name two professional conferences or associations you would like to join/attend.

Exercise 1 Additional Career Interests

What additional classes might be helpful to you when you start working in your new job? Name at least three classes.

1. _____

2. _____

3. _____

Changes in Employment Status

As you begin meeting your stated career goals, establish new ones. If you are following your life plan, you will have the desire to change jobs as you advance in your area of expertise. If and when this job change occurs depends upon many factors. Some reasons for changing jobs include a(n):

- Acquired experience for an advanced position
- Opportunity for higher salary
- Desire for improved work hours
- Need for increased responsibility, status, and/or power
- Perceived decrease in stress
- Desire for different work environment and/or colleagues

It is normal for employees to move within and outside of their company. A poor economy forces some employees to change positions and, in some cases, careers. Changes in employment status include promotions, voluntary terminations, involuntary terminations, lateral transfers, and retirement. The following section presents and discusses these changes in employment status and provides tips on how to handle each situation in a proactive and professional manner.

New Job Searches

Depending on their work situation, some employees determine that they must find a new job immediately, while other employees are constantly exploring opportunities. No matter your situation, identify when to share your desire for a new job and when to keep your job search private. If you have recently received a college certification or degree that qualifies you for a higher position, approach your supervisor or human resource department to inform the appropriate individuals of your increased qualifications and desire for additional responsibilities and/or promotion. It is also appropriate to share your need to change jobs if a situation is requiring you to move out of the area. In this instance, your employer may have contacts to assist you in securing a new job in another city. If you have had good performance evaluations and are leaving voluntarily, ask your immediate supervisor, another superior, or coworkers if they are willing to serve as references for future employers. If they agree to serve as references, secure letters of recommendation written on company letterhead. It is helpful to write and provide a draft letter for your reference that highlights your accomplishments and favorable work attitude. Finally, if you have mastered your job duties, have had good performance evaluations, and are beginning to feel bored, respectfully share your desire for increased responsibilities with your boss.

Apart from the previously mentioned circumstances, do not share your desire to change jobs with anyone at work. This includes close coworkers. Oftentimes, sharing secrets at work can be used against you. Therefore, keep your job search private. Conduct your job search outside of work hours and schedule job interviews before or after work.

Exercise 2   Employer Recommendations

List at least four key points to include in a draft letter of recommendation from your employer. Provide an example for each key point.

Key Point (Quality)	Example
1.	
2.	
3.	
4.	

Grace and style are two key words to remember if coworkers learn you are looking for a new position. When confronted about your job search, be brief and positive. State that you desire a move, be it the need for additional responsibility or the need for more money, but keep your explanation simple. You do not have to share details as to why you want to move on. It is also not necessary to share details about potential employers or the status of your job search.

Promotions

A **promotion** is when someone moves to a position higher in the organization with increased pay and responsibility. The first step in securing a future promotion within your company is to begin behaving and dressing for advancement. Secure a copy of the job description and/or research key skills necessary for your desired position. Begin acquiring work experience in the target area by volunteering for assignments that provide the needed experience. Develop new skills through appropriate classes, job training, and other educational experiences to increase your qualifications. Watch and learn from those who are already in the position you desire. Implement this plan and you will gain the necessary qualifications and have the experience when an advanced position becomes available.

If you receive a promotion, congratulate yourself. Your hard work has been noticed by others within your company, and they want to reward your excellent behavior. A promotion also means that you are advancing toward your career goals. When you are promoted, thank your former boss either verbally or with a simple handwritten thank-you note. Communicate to your former boss how he or she has helped you acquire new skills. Be sincere. Even if your former boss was less than perfect, his or her behavior taught you how to lead and manage. Keep your note positive and professional. With your promotion, you most likely will see an increase in pay, a new title, and new responsibilities. If your promotion occurred within the same company, do not gloat; there were probably others within the company who also applied for the job. Behave in a positive, pleasant, and professional manner that reinforces that your company made the right choice in selecting you for the position.

In your new job, do not try to reinvent the wheel. Become familiar with the history of your department or area. Be sensitive to the needs and adjustments of your new employees. Review files and begin networking with people who can assist you in achieving department goals. When you are new to a position, you do not know everything. Ask for and accept help from others.

With a history of favorable performance evaluations, Cory wants a promotion. Cory decided to take responsibility and began evaluating potential positions for which Cory might qualify. While conducting research, Cory created a list of additional knowledge, skills, and abilities needed for the promotion. Cory began taking classes, attending training seminars, and watching leaders within the company to prepare for a future promotion.

Voluntary Terminations

Leaving a job on your own is called a **voluntary termination.** Voluntary terminations frequently occur when an employee has taken a job with a new employer or when retiring. While at times the workplace can be so unbearable that you want to quit without having another job, it is best to not quit your job unless you have another job waiting. No matter what the situation, when voluntarily leaving a job, be professional and do not burn bridges.

When taking a voluntary termination, resign with a formal letter of resignation. A **letter of resignation** is a written notice of your voluntary termination. Unless you are working with a contract that specifies an end date of your employment, you are technically not required to provide advance notice of your voluntary termination. It is, however, considered unprofessional to resign from work and make your last day the same day you resign. Typically, two weeks' notice is acceptable. State your last date of employment in your letter of resignation. Include a positive statement about the employer and remember to sign and date your letter. Figure 1 is a sample letter of resignation.

In your final days of employment, do not speak or behave negatively. Leave in a manner that would make the company want to rehire you tomorrow. Coworkers may want to share gossip or speak poorly of others, but you must remain professional. It is also inappropriate to damage or take property that belongs to the company. Do not behave unethically. Take only personal belongings, and leave your workspace clean and organized for whoever assumes your position. Preserve the confidentiality of your coworkers, department, and customers.

February 1, 2015

Susie Supervisor
ABC Company
123 Avenue 456
Anycity, USA 98765

Re: Notice of Resignation

Dear Ms. Supervisor:

While I have enjoyed working for ABC Company, I have been offered and have accepted a new position with another firm. Therefore, my last day of employment will be February 23, 2012.

In the past two years, I have had the pleasure of learning new skills and of working with extremely talented individuals. I thank you for the opportunities you have provided me and wish everyone at ABC Company continued success.

Sincerely,

Jennie New-Job

Jennie New-Job
123 North Avenue
Anycity, USA 98765

Figure 1

Cory had a coworker who had been looking for a job over the past few months. Cory knew this because the coworker not only told everyone, but used the company equipment to update and mail her résumé. Cory often heard the coworker talking to potential employers on the telephone. On the day Cory's coworker finally landed a new job, the coworker proudly announced to everyone in the office that she was "leaving the prison" and that afternoon would be her last day at work. The coworker went on to bad-mouth the company, her boss, and several colleagues. As she was cleaning out her desk, Cory noticed that the coworker started packing items that did not belong to her. When Cory shared this observation, the coworker said she deserved the items and that the company would never miss them. A few weeks later, Cory's former coworker came by the office to say hello. Cory asked her how her new job was going. "Well…" said the coworker, "the job fell through." The coworker explained that she was stopping by the office to see if she could have her old position back. Unfortunately, the former coworker left in such a negative manner that the company would not rehire her.

On the last day of employment with your company, you may meet with a representative from the human resource department or with your immediate supervisor to receive your final paycheck. This paycheck should include all unpaid wages and accrued vacation. This is also when you will formally return all company property, including your keys and name badge. You may receive an

exit interview. An exit interview is when an employer meets with an employee who is voluntarily leaving a company to identify opportunities for improving the work environment. During this interview, a company representative will ask questions regarding the job you are leaving, the boss, and the work environment. The company's goal is to secure any information that provides constructive input on how to improve the company. Share opportunities for improvement, but do not turn your comments into personal attacks. While it is sometimes tempting to provide negative information in the interview, remain positive and professional.

Involuntary Terminations

Talk It Out

If you were to be laid off, what are the first three things you would do, and why?

Involuntary terminations are when you lose your job against your will. Types of involuntary terminations include **firing,** which happens when you are terminated because of a performance issue; a **layoff,** which is a result of the company's financial inability to keep your position; or a restructuring, which is when the company has eliminated your position due to a change in strategy.

If you are fired, you have lost your job as a result of a performance issue. Unless you have done something outrageous (such as blatant theft or harassment), you should have received a poor performance warning prior to being fired. Typically, this progressive discipline includes a verbal and/or written warning prior to termination. If you are totally unaware of why you are being fired, ask for documentation to support the company's decision. Firing based on outrageous behavior will be supported by a policy, while any performance issue should be supported with prior written documentation. When you are informed of your firing, you should immediately receive your final paycheck. You will also be asked to return all company property on the spot (including keys and name badge). Do not damage company property. Doing so is not only immature, but punishable by law. While you may be angry or caught off guard, do not make threats against the company or its employees. Remain calm and professional. If you think you are being wrongfully terminated, your legal recourse is to seek assistance from your state's labor commission or a private attorney.

Many people consider a layoff a form of firing. This is not true. Firing is a result of poor performance. A layoff is a result of a company's change of strategy or its inability to financially support a position. While some companies lay off employees based upon performance, most do it on seniority. Frequently, when the company's financial situation improves, employees may be recalled. A **work recall** is when employees are called back to work after being laid off. If you have been laid off, remain positive and ask your employer for a letter of reference and job-search assistance. This job-search assistance may include support with updating a résumé, counseling, job training, and job leads. Some companies require employees to take unpaid work days, called **furloughs.** Employees are required to take these unpaid work days. Work furloughs are not a result of poor performance. They are a result of employers trying to save financial resources. If your company implements a work furlough program, make the best of the situation. Be happy you still have a job, and find ways to assist the company in improving

Talk It Out

What is the best way to use your time during a furlough day?

its financial situation. Knowing your current employer is experiencing economic challenges provides you an opportunity to update your résumé and create a plan should your employer need to take additional steps toward saving resources.

In today's competitive environment, it is common for companies to restructure. **Restructuring** involves a company changing its strategy and reorganizing resources. This commonly results in eliminating unnecessary positions. If your position is eliminated, remain positive and inquire about new positions. In a restructuring situation, it is often common for new positions to be created. Once again, do not bad-mouth anyone or openly express your anger or dissatisfaction over the situation. If you have recently acquired new skills, now is the time to communicate and demonstrate them. Keep a record of your workplace accomplishments, and keep your ears open for new positions for which to apply.

Other Moves Within the Organization

In addition to promotions and terminations, there are several other methods of moving within and outside the company. These include lateral moves, demotions, and retirement. A **lateral move** is when you are transferred to another area of the organization with the same level of responsibility. Lateral moves involve only a change in department or work area. A change in pay is not involved in a lateral move. If you are moved to a different position and experience a pay increase, it is considered a promotion. If you are moved to a different position and experience a pay decrease, you have been demoted. While **demotions** are rare, they can occur if one's performance is not acceptable but the employee chooses to not leave the company. Of all the changes an employee can make, a demotion is by far the most difficult. You experience not only a decrease in pay, but also a decrease in job title and status. If you are demoted, remain professional and be respectful of your new boss.

The final change in employment status is called **retirement.** Retirement is when you are voluntarily leaving your employment and will no longer be working. Although this text addresses those entering the workforce, it is never too early to start planning for your retirement, both mentally and financially. This can be done by establishing career goals and deadlines, in addition to contributing to a retirement fund.

Entrepreneurship

Some individuals do not want to work for others and have a desire to be their own boss. A final and common form of career transition is that of becoming an entrepreneur. An **entrepreneur** is someone who assumes the risk of succeeding or failing in business through owning and operating a business. While owning and operating your own business may sound glamorous, doing so involves work. Individuals become entrepreneurs for several reasons. The most common reason is when someone has identified a business

Web Quiz

Take this web quiz or find another online quiz to identify if entrepreneurship is for you

http://www.sba.gov/ smallbusinessplanner/plan/ getready/SERV_SBPLANNER_ ISENTFORU.html opportunity he or she wants to exploit. People also become entrepreneurs because they would rather work for themselves, want more control of their work environment, want more income, or have lost their jobs and have been unable to find another.

Individuals with full-time jobs sometimes supplement their income by running a business on the side. It is unethical to run a side business that competes with or utilizes your employer's resources or confidential information. If your current employer allows employees to run side businesses, do not allow your side business to interfere with your full-time employment. Keep the two ventures separate.

Entrepreneurship is a rewarding career option for many and plays a valuable role in the U.S. economy. There are various methods of becoming an entrepreneur. You can start your own business, purchase an existing business, or operate a franchise. From a home-based business to running a chain of retail sites, every entrepreneur started with a dream. To be a successful entrepreneur, you need to have a passion for your business. You also need to know how to plan, manage finances, and make yourself creatively and professionally stand out from a crowd. These are all skills you have started to develop by reading this text.

If you are interested in becoming an entrepreneur, there are many resources available to you. Start by exploring the Small Business Administration website at www.sba.gov. Here you will find online, local, and national resources to get you started on the road to entrepreneurial success.

Talk It Out

What kind of business would you like to own? What steps would you need to take to make this occur?

Career Success

As you have learned, there are several methods of advancing your career both within and outside of an organization. Although it is not good to change jobs too frequently, those with healthy careers move and rarely stay in one position their entire career. Personal issues frequently influence the choices we make in our careers. Health matters, changes in marital status, children, and elder care are just a few of these issues. There is a French proverb that states that some work to live, while others live to work. While there are trade-offs, your personal life must be a priority. Any change in your career will not only affect you, but those to whom you are close. Therefore, make them a consideration in your career decisions.

Career success is all about personal choice and maintaining an attitude of success. Regardless of when you plan to advance your career, keep your résumé updated, make a commitment to continuous learning, and display leadership. Doing so keeps you motivated to take on additional responsibilities and increases your knowledge, skills, and abilities. This will prepare you if some unforeseen opportunity comes your way. Keep focused on your life plan and consistently display professionalism. By consistently displaying professionalism, you will possess skills that position you for a lifetime of workplace success.

Workplace Dos and Don'ts

Do continually update your skills and knowledge through training and development	*Don't* assume additional skills and knowledge are not necessary for advancement
Do keep an open mind for job advancement opportunities	*Don't* openly share your dissatisfaction for your current job
Do write a formal resignation letter when leaving a company and a thank-you note to a boss or mentor when receiving a promotion	*Don't* leave your job abruptly without providing adequate notice to your current employer
Do behave professionally when leaving a position	*Don't* take or ruin company property when leaving a position
Do provide valuable feedback and opportunities for improvement during an exit interview	*Don't* turn an exit interview into a personal attack on your former boss or coworkers

Concept Review and Application

Summary of Key Concepts

- Continue learning new skills to help reach your career potential
- Formal learning is another way to increase skills and knowledge
- Changes in employment status include promotions, voluntary terminations, involuntary terminations, lateral moves, and retirement
- Be cautious about sharing your desire for a new job
- There are two types of terminations: voluntary and involuntary
- When leaving voluntarily, submit a letter of resignation
- When leaving in an involuntary manner, do not burn bridges or behave in an unprofessional or unethical manner
- There is a difference between being fired and being laid off
- It is never too early to begin planning for your retirement
- Becoming an entrepreneur is an additional form of career transition

Key Terms

continual learning

entrepreneur

formal learning

involuntary
  termination

restructuring

voluntary termination

demotion

exit interview

furlough

lateral move

letter of resignation

retirement

work recall

development

firing

informal learning

layoff

promotion

training

If You Were the Boss

1. Why would it be important to encourage training and development sessions within your department?
2. You hear through the grapevine that one of your best employees is looking for another job. What should you do?
3. Management has told you that you must lay off four of your employees. How do you determine whom to lay off and how best to tell them? How do you defend your decision?

Web Links

http://marciaconner.com/intros/informal.html
http://careerplanning.about.com/od/quittingyourjob
http://www.insiderreports.com/bizltrs/resign1.htm

Activities

Activity 1

Identify additional training, development, and continual learning you will need for professional success.

Training	Development	Continual Learning

Activity 2

Identify your ideal job. What continual learning will you need to secure this job?

Job Move	Continual Learning

Activity 3

Name at least five ways you can begin to develop additional skills for a future promotion.

1. _____

2. _____

3. _____

4. _____

5. _____

Activity 4

Name at least three things you can do to decrease your chances of being laid off if that becomes necessary within your company.

1. _____

2. _____

3. _____

Activity 5

Write a draft letter of reference for yourself.

_____

_____

_____

_____

_____

_____

_____

1. To make you more diverse in your skills, attend _____ and

   _____.

2. The process of increasing knowledge in your career area is referred to as _____

   and _____.

3. Changes in employment status include promotions, _____ terminations,

   involuntary _____, lateral moves, and _____.

4. If you have had positive performance evaluations and are leaving voluntarily, secure a

   _____.

5. A/An _____ is a written notice of your voluntary termination.

6. Your _____ should include all unpaid wages and _____.

7. Employees who are _____ are terminated due to a/an

   _____ issue.

8. Employees who are _____ are terminated due to the company's

   _____.

9. A/An _____ is when you are transferred to another area of the organization.
   A change in pay is not involved.

10. A/An _____ is someone who assumes the risk of _____ or

    _____ through owning and operating a _____.

Suggested Readings

Shanoff, B. "Departing with Dignity," *Waste Age* 38 (September 2007): 26–28.

McKenzie, M. "Exit Interviews," *Smart Business Atlanta* 7 (March 2010): 24.

Shea, T. E. "Getting the Last Word," *HR Magazine* 55 (January 2010): 24–25.

"The Changing Organizational Chart: Up Isn't the Only Way to Success," *Health Care Collector* 21 (January 2008): 8.

Elmer, V. "The Invisible Promotion," *Fortune* (February 7, 2011): 31–32.

Gurchiek, K. "Motivating Innovation," *HR Magazine* (September 2009): 31–35.

CQ MEGASKILL: GLOBAL CONSCIOUSNESS

Performance Skills

- Understanding globalization
- Increasing awareness of cultural differences
- Questioning assumptions
- Becoming a global communicator
- Recognizing ethnocentrism
- Practicing critical cultural relativism

- Showing respect for diverse world views
- Optimizing global teamwork
- Creating global Websites
- Avoiding culture shock
- Doing your homework

 REFLECT BEFORE READING

Experiences in other countries and with other cultures provide us with valuable insight into our own culture. Similarly, experiences at "home" can promote international understanding. Can you think of experiences in your life that promoted this kind of insight and understanding?

YOUR TURN

DIRECTIONS: Answer true or false.

_____ 1. Many perceptions of the United States throughout the world come from movies and television shows shown abroad.

_____ 2. Outside of the United States, describing yourself or another person as a "foreigner" is a good idea since people generally view this term favorably.

_____ 3. Business cards are used more frequently in the United States than in other parts of the world.

_____ 4. Good business is good business; if a business practice is successful in New York City or Los Angeles, it will be successful elsewhere.

(Note: See answers at the end of this chapter.)

INTRODUCTION

Tom, an employee of an educational tutoring firm in the United States is meeting a group of employees in India. His objective is to outsource tutoring. At their first meeting together, Tom tries to come across in a friendly and informal manner. He begins by telling the group he does not consider titles all that important, so people should feel free to just call him Tom. He then applies the training he received back in the States. Instead of telling them what to do, he asks them for feedback regarding how to make this business venture successful. "What are your ideas?" he says.

At this point, there is a long period of silence. When no one responds, he calls on an individual named Kanwar and asks him what he thinks. The other Indian employees give Tom a bewildered look. They cannot understand why Tom is asking these questions. If he needs to ask these questions, then he must not know. Their confidence in him is shaken.

Tom needs to rethink his approach. In India, it is usually expected that someone like Tom will present his ideas first. Then, brainstorming and decision making by the group follows. When they eventually issue their report, they will do so as a group.

The global marketplace is not some futuristic concept. It is here and now. Given the changing nature of the marketplace and workforce, our ability to be good, knowledgeable, and sensitive citizens of the world will go a long way toward enhancing our chances for success.

Global competition affords consumers the opportunity to choose the best available products and services from around the world. If we think of the world as a pool of potential customers, the numbers are mind boggling. Furthermore, U.S. employers are increasingly expanding their reach for talent. Workers throughout the world are competing with each other for more jobs and particularly for the best jobs.

Ask yourself if you have the skills to compete in this type of environment. More specifically, what skills do you have that will be an asset in the global marketplace? What skills do you need to develop in order to be competitive? What is the best way for you to acquire these skills? Lastly, why are these questions important to you and your future?

DID YOU KNOW?

David Smith, author of If the World Were a Village, *posits what the world would look like if it were shrunk to 100 people. The graphic in Figure 1 shows the diversity of this global village.*

UNDERSTANDING GLOBALIZATION

Globalization refers to the growing interdependence among people and cultures throughout the world. Instant messaging, e-mail, Web conferencing, and other technologies make it possible to communicate and collaborate across cultures and countries. Travel, economic and government policies, trade, outsourcing

Figure 1 • If the World Were a Village of 100 People

From Asia	
From China	
From India	
From Africa	
From the U.S.A.	
Speak Chinese	
Speak English	
Speak Hindi	
Are Christians	
Are Muslims	
Are Buddhists	
Are Jewish	
Are Males	
Are Females	

partnerships, education, and migration have been instrumental in creating a global marketplace. Nowadays, the global integration of economies makes it more and more difficult to talk about the German economy, the Chinese economy, or even the economy of many smaller countries such as Cuba.

Although events taking place in other continents may seem distant and irrelevant to us as individuals, they may have a profound effect on our lives. Similarly, changes in our daily lives, such as our buying habits, can affect the economies, cultures, and lives of people far away. More and more issues extend beyond a country's geographical boundaries, including environmental concerns, terrorism and security, availability of work, fuel and transportation costs, and online education.

YOUR TURN · · · · · · ──────────

What two recent international developments are impacting your lifestyle at the present?

1. _____

_____

2. _____

_____

Today, organizations large and small can become global in an instant with a computer and an Internet connection. IBM is just one of a growing number of companies that view *every* citizen in *every* country as a potential customer. Therefore, if you are an IBM employee, your customer base is made up of approximately 6.5 billion people who

- Communicate in more than 6,000 living languages, including Mandarin Chinese, Spanish, English, Hindi, Portuguese, Bengali, Russian, Japanese, and Standard German.

- Share a large number of different nationalities with different perspectives and goals.

- Have a median age of approximately 28 years.

- Have an average life expectancy at birth of about 65 years.

- Represent a large number of religions with unique practices and beliefs, including Christians, Muslims, Hindus, Buddhists, Sikhs, and Jews.[1]

Understanding globalization requires us to peel back layers of culture. Traveling to countries around the world acquaints us with outer, more visible layers such as foods, fashions, and significant historical events. Inner, more hidden layers take the form of values, everyday norms and customs, and body language.

By reading novels and other works by authors from other cultures, living and studying abroad, developing friendships with people who are vastly different from us, reflecting on diverse customs and points of view, and immersing ourselves in other cultures wherever we find ourselves, we can deepen our understanding and appreciation of globalization. As we immerse ourselves in other cultures, we expand our knowledge base with regard to the meaning of culture, the interconnectedness of cultures, and cultural similarities and differences throughout the world.

YOUR TURN   · · · · · · ——————

The International Programs Center of the U.S. Bureau of the Census provides continuous updated projections of the world's population. Access the "World POPClock Projection" on the Internet at **www.census.gov/ipc/www/popclockworld.html** to find the most recent estimate of the world's population.

Total World Population = _____ as of _____ (date).

WHAT IS GLOBAL CONSCIOUSNESS?

(?) Where Am I Now?

DIRECTIONS: For each statement, mark M (most of the time), O (often), S (sometimes), R (rarely), or N (never).

1. _____ In culturally diverse situations, both at home and abroad, I think and act flexibly.

2. _____ In culturally diverse situations, both at home and abroad, I am very confident in my ability to adjust to any situation.

3. _____ As a global communicator, I am aware of my body language and what it communicates from culture to culture.

4. _____ I understand how being globally conscious opens up all kinds of opportunities for me.

5. _____ When I find myself in a "new" cultural environment, I have an easy time socially interacting and adjusting.

With globalization taking hold, the costs of cultural misunderstandings and biases are increasing. As borders become less important for travel, trade, and the media, expanding our vision becomes imperative. Put another way, employers need workers who exhibit **global consciousness**, meaning the awareness, understanding, and skills necessary to adjust to different cultures. Globally conscious employees understand how globalization affects virtually every aspect of their work.

How might our global consciousness affect the way we do our job? At one U.S. company with ties to Singapore, workers reevaluated the scheduling of routine meetings due to differences in time zones. Websites, such as timeanddate.com, facilitate the process of checking time zones in different countries and cities. Instead of asking their coworkers in Singapore to get up in the middle of the night, meetings are now held at different times in order to periodically accommodate everyone's preferences.

UPS, which operates in more than 200 countries, has created a global trade curricula for all "UPSers." Given the global marketplace in which it operates, UPS seeks new hires who are

- Conversant in multiple languages.
- Sensitive to foreign cultures.
- Able to learn how to learn.
- Capable of managing complexity and uncertainty.

A lack of global consciousness makes it difficult for us to know what constitutes ethical behavior in different cultures. What is **ethical**, or those standards for determining what conduct is right and wrong, varies from one part of the world to another. A few years ago, a U.S. nuclear submarine collided with a Japanese high school training vessel. Eight Japanese died in the collision. Formal statements of regret from top government officials and the submarine commander, Scott Waddle, only fueled Japanese resentment and skepticism. Next, a written statement by Waddle, issued through the Japanese consulate in Hawaii, was viewed as too little, too late, and too formal.

Only after the commander offered a sincere apology in person to families of the victims was an international crisis averted. If this incident had taken place in the United States, counsel would have instructed the parties involved to exercise their constitutional right to remain silent because of legal liability issues. But in Japan, the ethical thing to do is an immediate, heartfelt, personal apology to the victim by the person at fault. Apologies from an official or third party are not sufficient.

TO LEARN MORE

Go to **www.worldcitizensguide.org.** Click on the tab "World Flags." You will see small icons for 120 countries. As you move your mouse over each icon, you are given an interesting fact about each country and the major languages spoken there. For example, if you mouse over Bangladesh, you will learn: "Some people here use their chins to point at things."

INCREASING AWARENESS OF CULTURAL DIFFERENCES

Some trainers who lead workshops on global cultural differences advise people to "assume difference instead of similarity." Why? Because we tend to assume similarity. Perhaps you use a red pen to write a suggestion to a coworker who is a native of China. Later, your supervisor informs you that the coworker was highly insulted by the note. The problem was not the message. Rather, it had to do with the color red. In her culture, using that color to write a note such as this means "I wish you would die."

Assuming difference, as well as assuming similarity, has its downside. If we focus too much on our cultural differences, we run the danger of ignoring the many commonalities that unite us. Among other things, we all send messages and have a need to be understood, all of us live in groups and classify people in categories, and each and every one of us possesses a culture. These are **cultural universals**, meaning those behaviors, values, and beliefs found in all cultures.

Making a habit of assuming difference or assuming similarity locks us into a mode of thinking. Global consciousness requires us to be more flexible. By developing our cultural intelligence, we learn to be sensitive to possible differences and similarities among cultures. Not if but when we fail to show this sensitivity, we need to learn from our mistakes. If we mistakenly suggest a steak dinner to visiting staff from India, neglect to inspect a business card from a Japanese associate before putting it in our pocket, or offend a colleague by using written documentation rather than more personal face-to-face communication, these cultural missteps do not make us bad people. Rather, they simply indicate we need to expand our global consciousness.

 Applied · · · · · ·

Companies in the United States frequently use focus groups for market research. Recently, one U.S. drug company considered marketing one of their products in Japan. Before launching this venture, the company wanted to find out more about their new client base. Marketing materials for this drug would be evaluated by assembling a focus group of physicians in Japan. Soon, it became evident that this marketing strategy would not work.

In Japan, hierarchy is very important. People lower in the chain of command are hesitant to question higher-ups. Therefore, if a senior doctor likes the marketing approach, other doctors are quick to agree. After some thought, it was decided that doctors would be questioned individually. By taking into account the norms of Japanese culture, the drug company gathered the feedback it needed.

YOUR TURN · · · · · · ▬▬▬▬▬

Increasingly, women in business need to be aware of cultural rules of etiquette. Quiz yourself on how a woman should respond to the following situations.

DIRECTIONS: Answer true or false.

_____ 1. In France, cheek-kissing is an acceptable way for a Frenchman to introduce himself to you.

_____ 2. In Russia, when walking into a place with theatre-type seating, it is inconsiderate to enter facing the stage.

_____ 3. In Italy, it is perfectly OK for two women to walk arm in arm in public.

_____ 4. In Switzerland, punctuality is not the norm.

_____ 5. In Japan, you should avoid showing strong emotions such as anger.

(Note: See answers at the end of the chapter)

QUESTIONING ASSUMPTIONS

As we develop our global consciousness, we learn to question our assumptions—and then ask certain questions. As an example, when meeting with foreign clients, do we assume that punctuality is valued? What constitutes inappropriate dress? If we give gifts, do we even think about the color of the gifts and what it might signify (see Table 1)?

Stereotypical assumptions about a nation's personality are far from the truth, yet they are pervasive and often unquestioned. A recent survey of almost 4,000 people in 40 countries revealed that people everywhere believe stereotypes about a nation's personality, even their own. The researchers, Robert McCrae and Antonio Terracciano, discovered that we form misconceptions based on a country's leadership, historical events, and personal encounters traveling abroad.

Table 1 • Looking Beyond My Assumptions

Assumptions @	Predominant View in U.S.	Examples from Other Countries
Appointments	Punctuality is valued; after all, "time is money."	Punctuality is not valued in many Middle Eastern countries such as Israel and Saudi Arabia. Making a client wait is standard practice.
Dress	Business attire varies from conservative suits and skirts to more informal wear. Accessories, such as leather briefcases and handbags, are common.	Wearing or carrying anything made of leather will be offensive to Hindu clients, who view cows as sacred. In Saudi Arabia, Muslim beliefs dictate very modest attire for women. High dress, especially necklines, long sleeves, and long skirts are appropriate.
Gifts	A wide range of gifts is permissible. Flowers of any color are a common way of showing appreciation. Alcohol is a common gift during the holiday season.	In Japan and China, white flowers are associated with funerals. In China, even the color of the wrapping paper is significant. Alcohol is illegal in Muslim countries.

For instance, we may think of Germans as aggressive, based on Germany's role in World War II. Or we may think of Swedes as being conscientious, but they are no more so than the rest of us according to the researchers' data.[2]

YOUR TURN • • • • • ——————————

Briefly explain each of the following sayings and what values it supports. Are these U.S. values? And are they universal values? Explain.

1. "Pick yourself up by your own bootstraps." _____

_____

_____

_____

2. "A rolling stone gathers no moss." _____

_____

_____

_____

3. "The nail that sticks up gets hammered down." _____

_____

_____

_____

4. "I scratch your back, you scratch mine." _____

_____

_____

_____

(*Note:* See answers on p. 100.)

BECOMING A GLOBAL COMMUNICATOR

Global consciousness allows us to reconsider our traditional thinking, interactions, and communication skills. Thinking of ourselves as citizens of the world helps us move beyond nationalistic boundaries. Pearce and Pearce talk about the process of becoming a **cosmopolitan communicator**; that is, understanding and responding to situations as worldly people. Instead of thinking of ourselves solely as Americans, Koreans, or Russians, we need to consider our ties to a larger, interdependent community.[3]

According to the U.S. Department of Education, 24,000 U.S. elementary and secondary students study Chinese. In contrast, more than 200 million Chinese children study English.

DID YOU KNOW?

Global communicators consider their audience. What if you speak English much more fluently than your audience? If this is the case, it is a good idea to use gestures and a lot of visual aids. Do not talk fast and avoid the use of slang. If translation is necessary, be careful.

Since some words have multiple meanings and those meanings vary from one context to another, a straight translation using software is apt to create misunderstandings. For example, one international company explained they were terminating employees. In translating statements in English to Chinese, the company issued a statement to the effect that it would execute employees.

With cyber global communications, becoming multilingual is an extremely valuable skill. Although English is the primary language of international business, people still prefer doing business in their native language. For this reason, companies are rapidly globalizing their Websites, in part by making their sites available in a wide variety of languages.

Becoming a global communicator involves becoming more informed about how and why people from different cultures communicate the way they do. Understanding the cultural context of communication is critical. In Japan and many other Asian countries, mail says something about the sender. Therefore, the quality of the printing or other things that might distinguish the mailing assume more importance than in the United States.

 Applied · · · · · ·

Roger Axtell, author of Gestures: The Do's and Taboos of Body Language Around the World, *shares a wealth of advice to increase the knowledge base of globally conscious business travelers. Axtell, former vice president of worldwide marketing for Parker Pen Company, focuses on gestures, greetings, and business protocol in general.*

As an example, he explains that the process of exchanging business cards takes on a different meaning in Japan. Upon receiving a business card, Axtell recommends looking at it closely rather than quickly putting it away. Because the card represents one's personal and professional identity, it should be treated with respect. When presenting your own card, Axtell suggests doing so with both hands and bowing slightly. The lettering on the business card should face the recipient.

YOUR TURN · · · · · ·

Global communicators pay attention to body language, and what it communicates from culture to culture.

Look at Figure 2. What do each of these gestures mean to you?

- In Iran, Greece, and Turkey, nodding your head up and down means just the opposite of what it means in the United States. It means no. Moreover, in these countries, a yes can be indicated by moving one's head from side to side (no in the United States).

- A two-handed handshake in Saudi Arabia would be highly offensive. The left hand is considered unclean since it is used for certain hygienic functions. Consequently, you should not touch someone with this hand.
- The A-OK in Germany is an obscene reference to one's anatomy; while in some South American countries it can mean "f——— you."
- In Australia, thumbs up is interpreted as "up yours."
- In Argentina, circling your finger around your ear means you have a telephone call.

Figure 2 • Body Language, Culture, and Meanings

Nodding head up and down

Two-handed shake

A-OK

Thumbs up

Circling finger around ear

RECOGNIZING ETHNOCENTRISM

YOUR TURN • • • • •

Imagine you are participating in a workshop on careers, CQ, and globalization. One of the participants states, "I am studying to be a physical therapy assistant. My job will be to rehabilitate people without regard for who they are. I will bring someone back to their highest functional capacity. It doesn't matter if they are from Honduras, Mexico, or Spain. I don't need this training."

Do you agree with the position taken by this individual? Explain.

_____

_____

_____

_____

Margo Monteith, a psychologist at the University of Kentucky, conducted a test in which she asked people to associate certain words with America and a fictitious country called Marisat. Under time pressure, Monteith found that people were inclined to connect words such as *sunrise*, *paradise*, and *loyal* to

America. On the other hand, Marisat was more easily associated with words such as *death*, *evil*, and *poison*. According to Monteith, our self-esteem is closely related to our group membership. By feeling our group or nationality is better, we feel better about ourselves.[4]

Ethnocentrism is the assumption that our way of doing things is right and therefore superior. Ethnocentrism is found throughout the world. Because of their ethnocentric behavior, travelers from the United States are sometimes viewed as insensitive, ignorant, and "full of themselves." In the 1950s, Lederer and Burdick coined the term *Ugly American* to describe people from the United States who travel the world thinking that their society is the most culturally advanced and civilized. Since U.S. values were considered superior, the Ugly American did not feel it was necessary to understand, much less appreciate other cultures.[5] Even today, this reputation survives. Many people in other parts of the world think of U.S. citizens as loud, boastful, and selfish.

Ethnocentrism is pervasive in the United States and elsewhere. For example, many of us think there is one universal or acceptable way of doing business, and that way is our way. If we encounter people who do not understand or practice our way, then we assume they are misguided, or we try to teach them how to become more like us.

Even the term *American* is ethnocentric. People in the United States use this term to describe only themselves, when in fact Americans populate the entire continents of North and South America. For this reason, I avoid using the term *Americans* to describe the population of the United States.

All humans share the same basic priorities in life: true or false? As we develop our cultural intelligence, it becomes increasingly clear why the answer is false. Culture influences how people judge what is most important. As an example, people in the United States tend to place more importance on individual priorities such as personal fulfillment and autonomy. Japanese, on the other hand, may sacrifice personal concerns for social acceptance. In contrast, Middle Eastern cultures often place a higher priority on reaching out to others and being hospitable.

 Where Am I Now?

When interacting with people from a country whose culture is very different from mine, I:

Might judge them by my own cultural standards.
Example:

_____

_____

_____

Might have a condescending attitude toward their lifestyles.

Example:

_____

_____

_____

Might assume they should do things just like I do.

Example:

_____

_____

_____

Might be unaware of my own cultural values.

Example:

_____

_____

_____

PRACTICING CRITICAL CULTURAL RELATIVISM

In contrast to ethnocentrism, cultural relativism does not assume that any one culture is perfect or always right. **Cultural relativism** maintains that any culture's values and beliefs must be understood on the basis of its own standards. In other words, we should not use our own standards to judge another culture.

Cultural relativism promotes understanding and tolerance. However, it has a downside. For example, **absolute cultural relativism** says we should not even question what takes place in another culture. To do so promotes ethnocentrism. However, what if we think the behavior in question harms people or violates their basic rights?

Another form of cultural relativism offers an alternative view. **Critical cultural relativism** poses questions about cultural beliefs and practices in an effort to understand better why they exist, who accepts them, and who they benefit or harm. When we employ critical cultural relativism, we evaluate all cultures, including our own, with the understanding that no culture is perfect. This allows us to respect and understand cultural differences and at the same time maintain a critical perspective.

In Trompenaars and Hampden-Turner's best-selling book, _Riding the Waves of Culture: Understanding Cultural Diversity in Business_, the authors discuss cultural differences that revolve around relationships with people. From their perspective, one of the most important is "universalism" versus "particularism." The universalist approach is founded on the idea that certain rules or contracts should be followed regardless of the circumstances. The particularist approach sees universalism as too rigid. It maintains that special circumstances and personal relationships take precedence over any abstract rule.

According to Trompenaars and Hampden-Turner, much of the research on universalism and particularism has been done in the United States. Perhaps this is why some researchers have concluded that all societies should emulate universalism, since this approach underlies business dealings in the United States.

However, the authors caution against assuming that any one approach is necessarily the best. They argue in favor of critical cultural relativism. By critiquing both approaches, we can see the advantages and pitfalls of each. For example, an employee based in the United States (universalist culture) might be conducting business with a supplier from Japan (particularist culture). For these employees to be successful, cultural self-awareness and flexibility are key skills. The U.S. employee might conclude that while a contract is necessary, putting too much emphasis on a contract might imply a lack of trust and limit flexibility. Similarly, the supplier from Japan might come to realize that contracts and personal relationships are both necessary and can even reinforce each other. In some situations a contract might be necessary, for without it, there might be confusion as to the exact nature of an agreement or what recourse is available if both sides do not uphold their end of the deal. By seeing the benefits and disadvantages of both approaches, it may be possible for these individuals to avoid the extremes of ethnocentrism and absolute cultural relativism by critically evaluating and integrating their cultural differences.

SHOWING RESPECT FOR DIVERSE WORLDVIEWS

Different cultures have different **worldviews**, frameworks for making sense of the world. Each day, we see and hear a smorgasbord of worldviews, relating to things such as religion, the universe, humanity, nature, or other philosophical issues that address who we are or our concept of being. For example, different worldviews exist regarding our relationship to nature. Many Asians and Native Americans emphasize unity with nature and reverence for nature. In other cultures, humanity and nature are seen as separate. To many North Americans, nature is something to overcome or control. However, in some African cultures, people believe that nature is beyond our control.

Whether or not we recognize it, these worldviews affect all aspects of culture, including our priorities, behaviors, and how we express ourselves. In a culture that attaches great importance to personal expressiveness, we are likely to observe people engaging in a wide variety of facial expressions and gestures. To offer another example, we would expect to find a great deal of emphasis on the *process* of communication in a culture that values harmonious group relations. In a culture such as this, the emotional exchange of communicating and the relationships communication gives rise to are apt to be valued as much as the end product of communication.

In spite of globalization, individuals may find themselves working in organizations that do not respect multiple worldviews. Fortunately, this is slowly changing as evidenced by recent corporate developments such as the following:

- Employees of a major airline in the United States are now allowed to wear turbans, yarmulkes, and hijabs as part of their uniform.

- A multinational power equipment maker which operates in 128 countries has rewritten its corporate statement of principles. It now reflects not just its traditional Lutheran values, but Muslim and other values as well.

- A large hotel in a major metropolitan area in the United States has set aside a room for its Muslim employees who need to pray several times during their shifts. This provides those employees with a private room in which to place their prayer rug when they pray towards Mecca.

CQ Applied

Cultural beliefs regarding modesty differ. In her research, Dr. Caryn Andrews found people's beliefs about modesty can affect health-care utilization. As an example, certain procedures, such as disrobing or having personal contact with a technician, might be at odds with tzeniut, the Hebrew belief in modesty. Research on other cultures, such as Muslims, Hispanics, Asians, and the Amish, show modesty can interfere with screenings, check-ups, and overall health care.

In order to study this issue in more detail, Dr. Andrews created a questionnaire to measure patient modesty. The result is a modesty scale, used by hospitals nationwide to measure degrees of modesty. By taking cultural modesty into account, providers show utmost respect and sensitivity.[6]

What are some ways in which health care providers are adapting? Solutions can be relatively simple, such as putting up a curtain or making it possible for the patient to cover her body while waiting for a provider. In some cases, hospitals now provide gowns that cover the entire body. When discussing private issues, providers can make sure the door is closed and ask the individual if he or she would like to have a family member or someone else present.

Respecting worldviews requires extra thought, knowledge, and sensitivity. If you are setting up a meeting in a multicultural workplace, numerous considerations are important. For example:

1. Does the scheduling of the meeting conflict with holidays, local festivities, or religious observances?

2. What are the attendees' cultural norms?
   - Should you get right down to business or first spend some time building rapport?
   - What are appropriate topics for getting to know each other?
   - What are the hours of a normal workday; and when is it OK to break for lunch?

3. What is the protocol for decision making?
   - Should you make information available before or during meetings?
   - Are decisions made by individuals or group consensus?
4. What is the structure of meetings?
   - Does everyone attend, or just certain people, such as implementers and/or evaluators?
   - Should people be seated randomly, by position, or in some other way?
5. What are the speaking norms?
   - Who opens the meeting? Who speaks first?
   - What gestures are taboo?

OPTIMIZING GLOBAL TEAMWORK

DID YOU KNOW?

In a recent survey of virtual global teams, the top three sources of problems reported by team members were:

1. Poor sharing of information.
2. Unclear or inappropriate expectations.
3. Unclear lines of accountability or control.[7]

Because of computer technology, work is becoming a thing we do rather than a place we go. As businesses expand throughout the world and as technologies facilitating collaborative work improve, global teams become more commonplace. The idea behind global teamwork is that people from countries and cultures worldwide will be better able to problem-solve and offer a variety of perspectives. While communication technologies such as e-mail, team rooms (members collaborate on a real-time basis), teleconferencing, and videoconferencing make virtual teamwork possible, they cannot eliminate problems caused by distance.

Even when members of teams know each other and can sit down in the same room and talk, efficient and productive teamwork is not necessarily easy. When team members live in different countries, talk different languages, and barely know each other, the challenges are formidable. The geographical and cultural distance separating team members creates a number of challenges besides the obvious ones of sharing information and cultivating team camaraderie and spirit.

Different needs and customs regarding team reward system. Rewards are things that motivate individuals and groups. If not tailored to the culture, rewards meant to motivate can actually alienate. As previously mentioned, some cultures do not want to bring attention to themselves as individuals; and therefore, seek to avoid individual rewards. In a situation such as this, acknowledging the efforts of a group in some manner might be more appropriate.

Cultural clashes. Misunderstandings may result from lack of awareness and respect for cultural expectations of dispersed team members.

Different work cultures may have different beliefs regarding decision making. Teams in some companies and regions of the world are more apt to follow top-down decision making. Elsewhere, there may be more input from people at different levels. If members of the same global team unknowingly employ different decision-making styles, it can seriously impair their ability to work together.

Lack of trust. As social distance increases or as interaction and familiarity decrease, there tends to be less trust. Generally, we are less apt, at least initially, to trust people with whom we do not identify. For example, consider who you would *not* welcome as family, close friends, coworkers, or neighbors. Now ask yourself: Would you trust these same people? Since trust is such a sensitive issue, we tend to ignore it.

Exclusion. Any perceived difference, especially if it is seen as important, can marginalize team members and create disunity. In a team, certain individuals may not feel included. One way of minimizing exclusion is to be responsible with the words and symbols we use to communicate. Anticipating multiple perspectives and reactions goes a long way toward tapping, sharing, and using everyone's input.

Meeting the challenges of global teamwork requires us to

- Seek agreement regarding team goals as well as individual roles and responsibilities.

- Make a concerted effort to stay in touch. For instance, you and other team members might agree to answer e-mails within 24 hours.

- Meet in person as much as possible in order to build trust and if necessary rebuild shattered trust. Kickoff meetings, celebrations of major milestones in a project, and discussions at critical junctures are good times to meet.

CREATING GLOBAL WEBSITES

At any given time, millions of people are using the Internet to shop, read the news, or research some subject. According to the *Computer Industry Almanac*'s recent estimate, more than 1 billion people worldwide use the Internet. Regardless of what people are looking for, they usually have little or no awareness of where the information they access originates. What matters is whether the information is personally and culturally relevant to them.

Given the nature of the Internet, any website is inherently global. Or is it? According to a recent Web Globalization Report Card, most Websites are lacking in terms of their worldwide reach and local usability.[8]

While Web globalization removes geography as a factor, the cultural comfort level of a Website provides a competitive edge. When content is in their native language, Web surfers stay at a site much longer. Additionally, consumers are much more likely to buy a product or service from a Website in their native language because they can research it more thoroughly.

What do the global Websites have in common? With one click, you can access the information you need in a variety of languages including your own. As an example, Google offers more than 100 different language interfaces, and more than half of Google's traffic comes from outside of the United States.

Furthermore, a Website should be culturally relevant. For instance, research on car buying habits shows how the appeal of certain vehicles and even the process of buying those cars varies from culture to culture. A global Website utilizes this information in tailoring its content to different cultures.

TO LEARN MORE

Go to the BBC homepage at **www.bbc.co.uk/languages**, home of the British Broadcasting Company on the Internet. You will be able to read or hear the news in 33 languages. Visit the BBC interactive Website, "Your Voice" at **www.bbc.co.uk/voices/yourvoice.** It was recently named the Best Global Website. BBC's "Your Voice" Website promotes and creates cross-cultural dialogue on topics such as language ecology, language and age, why study language, and when languages collide. You will be asked to share your point of view on these topics and many more, or put your questions to an expert and join the discussion.

YOUR TURN · · · · ·

Surf the Internet and find a corporate Website that you would rate as excellent in terms of its global reach, and one that you would rate as poor. Compare and contrast the two Websites, as you explain the reasons behind your ratings.

_____
_____
_____
_____
_____
_____
_____
_____
_____

MINIMIZING CULTURE SHOCK

Culture shock, the disorientation we feel when we encounter a significantly different way of life, is a two-way street. We may inflict culture shock on someone else when we do things that offend and alienate others. Additionally, we may be on the receiving end of culture shock when we come face to face with a radically different lifestyle. While we can experience culture shock at home, it tends to be most intense when traveling abroad or returning home after a long absence.

When we find ourselves in an unfamiliar environment, our expectations may not mesh with our actual experiences. This may be due to the influence of the media. As an example, we may experience culture shock upon learning that Australians do not necessarily dress like Crocodile Dundee. Or we may expect all Chinese to know martial arts, all Africans to live in huts in villages, and all Americans to be rich.

Culture shock can take its toll on us. It can make us feel anxious, disoriented, and depressed. We may lose confidence in our ability to socially interact and adapt in new situations. Another consequence is dissatisfaction with the "new" environment and the way people behave. In some cases, culture shock can strain and even ruin relationships.

Minimizing culture shock requires new knowledge and insights as well as a certain degree of flexibility. It is counterproductive to simply think in terms of specific do's and don'ts when visiting a country or region. No one source of information can cover all possibilities. Within a culture, everyone and every group has specific habits, expectations, and norms. Consequently, you will encounter situations that have no script; situations that go beyond previously learned routines. When in doubt, it is wise to follow a saying that comes from Columbia. It says, "When visiting, try to behave the way others behave."

To minimize the likelihood of culture shock, keep in mind the following:

- *Learn what questions to ask and listen actively.* Are there certain conversational topics to avoid? How do people behave at social gatherings? What kinds of gestures are considered offensive?

- *Try to expand and diversify your network.* If possible, develop relationships with males and females of various cultural backgrounds and mentors with international business experience.

- *Conduct environmental scans.* Pay careful attention to the behavior of others as well as the cultural context, status of people, and formality of the situation. For instance, closely observe introductions, eye contact, behaviors toward men and women, and deference toward people in authority.

- *Remember the possible pitfalls of humor.* What is funny to you might be rude or offensive to someone from another culture. If in doubt, do not take a chance.

- *Recognize the importance of humility.* Don't assume that you are better or more able because of your background, education, or credentials. By staying humble, you show that you do not know it all. Rather, you leave room for communication and show that you want to learn and grow.

Minimizing cultural shock is a process. Developing our global consciousness allows us to move beyond confusion and paralysis of action to acceptance and adjustment.

DOING YOUR HOMEWORK

Usually, failures in international business are not due to technical or professional incompetence. According to research, most failures stem from an inability to adapt to diverse ways of thinking and acting. Think about it. Employees living in the United States equip themselves with a vast array of knowledge before they attempt to conduct business. Market research provides them with the latest data on the needs, values, and buying habits of consumers in the United States. Yet, when businesspeople venture into the international arena, they are often woefully unprepared. Whether they deal with managers, fellow workers, or customers, they display a lack of knowledge that would be totally unacceptable at home. Almost unconsciously, we tend to take our own cultural habits and norms with us when we travel abroad and project what we learn "at home" onto others.

Before entering into a business relationship with persons from another country, it is helpful to do your homework. Acquaint yourself with the country's culture, and not just the business, technological, and political sectors. All social institutions, such as education, family, and religion, impact how we interact and conduct business. For instance, a country's religious philosophy or spirituality can further one's understanding of why people behave the way they do. When doing business with an organization, it is important to understand its culture, including its values, norms, beliefs, language, and symbols. Information should be current since organizations change constantly.

Culture-specific information may be obtained from intercultural business consultants as well as foreign chambers of commerce, embassies, or other respected representatives of a particular country or group. Avoid quick and easy guides to travel in foreign countries. Often, information of this nature is full of sweeping generalizations that promote misunderstandings.

Go online to search for information about music, literature, history, and anything that might provide you with insight into a country's values, beliefs, and language(s).

For those interested in educational opportunities, international education programs are offered at the high school and college level. Additionally, there are internship exchanges, study tours, and training seminars and conferences available through a variety of government, business, and educational organizations worldwide. Some opportunities include scholarships, internships, and volunteer positions.

According to a recent survey on global relocation of workers, 81% of organizations offered cross-cultural training before assignments took effect. Interestingly, only 20% said this training was required. A sizable majority (73%) indicated cross-cultural training programs had high value. However, only 29% reported that CD-based and Web-based programs had high value.[9]

TO LEARN MORE

Access the Global Policy Network (GPN) Website at **http://gpn.org/main1.html**. GPN provides information to the public on working people in the global economy. In particular, it provides up-to-date statistical information and analysis on a growing number of countries. View the information on a country about which you know very little. How might this information help you as a business traveler to this country?

THE BOTTOM LINE

Globalization is infusing cultural differences into our everyday existence. This is even true for those of us who will live most if not all of our lives in the vicinity of our place of birth. Consequently, global consciousness is a necessary megaskill, in that it represents one of the most important and fundamental abilities we will have to develop in the 21st century. In addition to enabling us to cross cultural boundaries with ease, work with others, and see the value of multiple perspectives and experiences, global consciousness will allow us to pursue exciting and well-paying employment opportunities.

As previously discussed, lack of attention to cultural differences can have dire consequences, both at home and abroad. Research shows that international business ventures fail more because of a lack of global consciousness than professional or technical incompetence. With the emergence of an information economy in the United States, there is a need for culturally sensitive knowledge workers. White-collar jobs now place a premium on understanding cultures, languages, business practices, and world affairs. If workers cannot appreciate how our way of life is intertwined with the economic fortunes of the rest of the world, they become a liability.

By enhancing our awareness, understanding, and skills, global consciousness impacts the bottom line. As one key component of cultural intelligence, global consciousness allows us to excel in new and emerging environments that require flexibility, understanding, and the ability to appreciate the talents and contributions of all people and cultures.

A Look Back: I Have Learned

✓ _____ What is meant by globalization.

✓ _____ How globalization is changing our lives.

✓ _____ Why global consciousness is a megaskill today.

✓ _____ The value of becoming a global communicator.

✓ _____ How we can develop our global consciousness.

✓ _____ How to question our assumptions.

✓ _____ How to recognize ethnocentrism.

✓ _____ What is meant by critical cultural relativism.

✓ _____ How to show respect for diverse worldviews.

✓ _____ How global teamwork offers challenges and opportunities.

✓ _____ How to avoid or minimize culture shock.

✓ _____ How and why global consciousness impacts the bottom line.

Individual Action Plan

Think about one specific thing you can do to improve your skills in the area of global consciousness. Then complete the following plan during the next _____ (state time period).

Specific skill I want to improve first (refer to list of Performance Skills at the beginning of the chapter):

_____

My strategy:

_____

_____

_____

_____

_____

In order to develop this skill, I will:

_____

_____

_____

_____

Possible obstacles include:

_____

_____

_____

_____

Resources I need:

_____

_____

_____

_____

I will measure my progress by:

_____

_____

_____

_____

Answers

Your Turn (*see the beginning of the chapter*)

_____ 1. Many perceptions of the United States throughout the world come from movies and television shows shown abroad. (*True*) For example, American women are perceived to be uniformly glamorous, sexy, and promiscuous. Women working abroad might need to counter this image by dressing conservatively and acting professionally in all business dealings. In general, the more women know, the less important gender becomes.

_____ 2. Outside of the United States, describing yourself or another person as a "foreigner" is typically a compliment. (*False*) Actually, it is a good idea to avoid using the term altogether. In many languages, such as French and Spanish, the word *foreigner* suggests something strange or alien. A better word to use is *international*.

_____ 3. Business cards are used more frequently in the Unites States than in other parts of the world. (*False*) Business cards, which are almost ritually exchanged in many countries, provide a record of the people you meet and how to contact them. In some countries, there is formal protocol regarding exchanging cards.

_____ 4. Good business is good business; if a business practice is successful in New York City or Los Angeles, it will be successful elsewhere. (*False*) Numerous examples show this line of reasoning to be faulty. Ignoring cultural differences may very well jeopardize business transactions abroad. Greeting others by shaking hands, holding eye contact, avoiding social chit-chat, and observing the importance of punctuality are typically the norm in New York City. These behaviors might be deviant and even offensive in cities in the Middle East, China, and other parts of the world.

Your Turn: Cultural Rules of Etiquette for Women (*see the section, Increasing Awareness of Cultural Differences*)

1. In France, cheek-kissing is an acceptable way for a Frenchman to introduce himself to you. (*False*) Cheek-kissing is normally limited to good friends. If you shake hands with a Frenchman, however, he may slowly draw you closer and give you an "air kiss" to the one or both cheeks.

2. In Russia, when walking into a place with theatre-type seating, it is inconsiderate to enter facing the stage. (*True*) Enter with your back to the stage. By doing this, people you are passing will not see your rear.

3. In Italy, it is perfectly OK for two women to walk arm in arm in public. (*True*) This is simply a sign of friendship. It is not uncommon to see two men walking arm in arm as well.

4. In Switzerland, punctuality is not the norm. (*False*) You are expected to be on time. A widely known joke states that someone who arrives late does not wear a Swiss watch.

5. In Japan, you should avoid showing strong emotions such as anger. (*True*) Japanese are taught to control their emotions. Therefore, gesturing wildly or losing one's temper is viewed as impolite.

Your Turn: Analysis of Values Exercise (*see the section, Questioning Assumptions*)

1. "Pick yourself up by your own bootstraps" is a popular saying in the United States. It emphasizes independence and individualism. Contrast this saying with an African proverb, "It takes a whole village to raise a child."

2. "A rolling stone gathers no moss" emphasizes the U.S. preoccupation with mobility and speed. The Japanese have a similar saying, but the meaning is quite different. Moss represents important traditions. If people are constantly on the move, they will not appreciate those traditions and consequently they lose something of great value in the process.

3. "The nail that sticks up gets hammered down." This is a Japanese proverb. Contrast it with the popular saying in the United States, "The squeaky wheel gets the grease."

4. "I scratch your back, you scratch mine." In the United States, this means if you help me, I'll help you. Contrast this saying with the concept of giving in other cultures, in which nothing is expected in return. This even applies to giving something priceless to a total stranger.

Notes

1. CIA – The World Factbook. Online 7/18/2005. Available at **http://cia.gov/cia/publications/factbook/geos/xx.html**.

2. Dennis O'Brien, "Americans, Canadians Really Are Like Two Peas in a Pod," *Baltimore Sun*, October 21, 2005, pp. 1D + .

3. W. Barnett Pearce and Kimberly Pearce, "Extending the Theory of the Coordinated Management of Meaning (CMM) through a Community Dialogue Process," *Communication Theory, 10*(4), 2000, pp. 405–424.

4. Shankar Vedantam, "Psychiatry Ponders Whether Extreme Bias Can Be an Illness," *Washington Post*, December 10, 2005, pp. A1 + .

5. W. J. Lederer and E. Burdick, *The Ugly American* (New York: Norton, 1958).

6. Stephanie Shapiro, "Medicine and Modesty," *Baltimore Sun*, March 11, 2005, pp. 1E + .

7. Lindsley Boiney, "Gender Impacts Virtual Work Teams." Online 7/25/2005. Available: **http://gbr.pepperdine.edu/014/teams/html**.

8. John Yunker, *The Web Globalization Report Card 2005* (San Diego, CA: Byte Level Research, 2005).

9. GMAC Global Relocation Services, *2006 Global Relocation Trends Survey* (Woodridge, IL: 2006).

Index